CRAFT BREW

RED ⚡ LIGHTNING BOOKS

CRAFT BREW

AN AMERICAN BEER REVOLUTION

M. B. MOONEY

This book is a publication of

Red Lightning Books
1320 East 10th Street
Bloomington, Indiana 47405 USA
redlightningbooks.com

Manufactured in the United States of America

First printing 2021

Library of Congress Cataloging-in-Publication Data

Names: Mooney, M. B., author.
Title: Craft brew : an American beer revolution / M. B. Mooney.
Description: Bloomington, Indiana, USA : Red Lightning Books, 2021. |
    Includes bibliographical references.
Identifiers: LCCN 2021018601 (print) | LCCN 2021018602 (ebook) | ISBN
    9781684351558 (hardback) | ISBN 9781684351565 (paperback) | ISBN
    9781684351572 (ebook)
Subjects: LCSH: Beer festivals—United States—Guidebooks. |
    Microbreweries—United States—Guidebooks.
Classification: LCC GT2890 .M67 2021 (print) | LCC GT2890 (ebook) | DDC
    394.1/30973—dc23
LC record available at https://lccn.loc.gov/2021018601
LC ebook record available at https://lccn.loc.gov/2021018602

CONTENTS

ACKNOWLEDGMENTS

Neither this book, nor the previous one I wrote about beer fests, would have been possible without some amazing people who led me in the right direction and gave me an inside look into the craft brew culture.

To the great friends and homebrewers who shared their homemade brews with me—Scott Freed, Steven Faletti, Bill Hawkins, and Walt Wooden—your friendship and patience with a new convert welcomed me and taught me a great deal.

To Phil Ferril, the brewmaster with experience at beer fests, homebrewing, and the changes in craft beer over the decades, your insight and knowledge were invaluable.

To the brewers and owners I've had the pleasure of interviewing, you were all a pleasure to talk to and generous with your time and stories. Every conversation only confirmed the amazing character of the individuals within the craft beer industry.

I also want to thank Indiana University Press. You have been professional and kind in dealing with a strange author publishing for the first time.

My agent, Cyle Young, helped me get this opportunity and answered my dumb questions. You and the Serious Writer community—notably Bethany Jett and Michelle Medlock Adams—have overwhelmed me with support and direction on all the details of the publishing industry.

When we got married, my wife, Becca, promised that she would always invest in my dreams, and she has never wavered. I don't deserve you, and you give new meaning to "out of my league." I'm thankful God helped me find a partner to live this great adventure with.

CRAFT BREW

INTRODUCTION

America has a complicated history with beer.

William Shakespeare wrote, "A quart of ale is a dish for a king," but many Americans associate beer with the working class rather than the well-to-do. They believe it causes trouble because people guzzle it as a cheap way to get inebriated.

A puritanical religious heritage, well-meaning but misguided reformers, and a dash of anti-immigrant hostility against the Irish and Germans led our nation to pass a law—an amendment to the Constitution itself—that outlawed alcohol. This required a two-thirds majority of the US House and Senate.

Rampant crime and violence convinced lawmakers that this "noble experiment" did not solve society's ills but rather exacerbated them to an exponential degree. The US changed the Constitution again in 1933.

As difficult as it is to pass an amendment to the US Constitution, changing minds or culture is even harder. The negative attitudes toward alcohol, and especially beer, remained. The big conglomerates underscored this mentality by selling cheap, watery, low-quality beer across America, pumping massive amounts of money into advertising and keeping small breweries out of the market.

Enter the craft beer revolution.

An underground movement to make great beer began during the larger counterculture revolution of the sixties and seventies. A young generation rebelled against the greed and consumerism that the previous generation celebrated. A small section of those young men and women simply sought to have beer they liked to drink, which was cheaper overall and of higher quality. In that historical context, groups of homebrewers gathered and started making beer. Through practice and passion, they eventually made great beer.

Laws needed to be changed, but the craft movement didn't see those changes as purely, or even primarily, political. It sought freedom to be innovative and excellent at brewing beer. The craft brewers didn't believe that changing the laws would change the culture, however. America had already proven that didn't work.

The craft brewers worked to change the dominant perceptions of beer by doing things differently and by creating another option. They showed that beer can be different, with a unique hearkening back to the past, such as German social houses combined with American innovation. People aren't forced or coerced into the craft community. They are invited and welcomed and told there's a place for everyone.

As a descendent of those Irish and German immigrants in the mid-nineteenth century, that movement fascinates and inspires me. I'm not alone. Craft beer is an industry with a message.

Craft beer converts you with better-quality beer and a celebration of experiences rather than products. Each brewery's unique personality and style is a treasure in your town or neighborhood.

Instead of crushing the competition, the business model is to be collaborative and generous for the good of all those in the industry.

Brewers are part head chef and part mad scientist, and they'll tell you the stories behind their creations.

Local breweries are community centers with long tables. They invite neighbors to be friends first and customers second, and they give generously to local charities.

Craft brewing is an industry about relationships and personal interactions. It's about slowing down and taking a moment to make a new friend or reconnect with an old one. It's not about getting drunk but about having one or two brews, enjoying them and the company, and getting home safely.

And it's about great beer.

After years of unparalleled growth, even during the economic crisis that began in 2008, the craft industry is going through a transition. The founders and legends of the sixties and seventies are retiring and passing on. Will the inspiring culture survive? Will the next generation share the same message?

Because craft beer is a people's movement, I've interviewed several brewers and owners of breweries all around the country. A few of these breweries opened within the last few years. Others have been around for more than a decade. A couple opened in states where laws only recently became more favorable to local breweries. Others opened in states where there's a brewery in every small town.

The craft culture has its founding principles, but there is a great deal of diversity and individuality within those ideals. Each brewery in this book has its own perspective and experience.

I have included one very brief chapter on the history of beer and craft brewing as a context for the discussion, but most of what follows is a conversation with people within the industry.

Imagine that we're sitting at a long table at a local brewery, each of us with a mug of a favorite brew or a flight to try some new beers, sharing stories and ideas about this craft beer movement, what it means to us, and what we think about it.

It starts with a beer that changed everything.

THE CONVERSION

Despite my Irish and German ancestry, I didn't drink beer as a young man.

There were a few reasons for this. Growing up in the evangelically religious South, I was raised with a negative view of drinking in general. It wasn't completely negative, though. I remember my dad bringing home airline bottles of whiskey, which my mom would keep on the top shelf in the cupboard. Anytime I got sick with a cold or congestion, she gave me a little shot of whiskey to clear up the phlegm and probably to help me rest.

I blazed my own path in our growing suburban Georgia—wearing long hair and rocking it out in heavy metal bands—so I was open to seeing what things in life were all about, alcohol included. But when I was faced with alcohol through friends and acquaintances, the experience only confirmed the negative view.

First, it tasted horrible. The prevailing term for beer in certain circles was "horse piss." My limited consumption proved that true. People told me I had to acquire a taste for it. That never made sense to me. Why drink something that tasted like crap so that you could learn to like crap? At that time, parties were about getting the cheapest beer possible, so you can imagine the quality.

Second, the people who drank mostly drank too much. The goal was getting drunk, and that meant getting sick or doing stupid things. Much of that can be attributed to youthful ignorance or exuberance, but seeing people vomit, or being the one who puked, didn't appeal to me, either.

Last, even though the beer was cheap, drinking in general was expensive for me. I had dreams for other things, mainly making it in music, and I funneled what little money I had into those dreams. By the time I got into college and could get into bars, even the sodas cost too much for me, much less wine or other types of drinks, some of which I did enjoy.

I didn't have a problem with others who spent their money on it and decided, for whatever reason, that drinking was important to them. I drank alcohol occasionally and in moderation. Often I'd be the designated driver. I just thought this drinking thing wasn't for me—especially beer. That was way down my list.

Until I was converted.

The first beer I drank that I could stomach was Rolling Rock. I just dated myself there, because Rolling Rock, a light American lager, was popular in the college scene in the early to mid-1990s. I didn't hate it. Looking back now, I know it wasn't great beer, but it paved the way for my conversion.

I've been drinking craft beer for years now, so it sounds cheesy to me, but Guinness turned me on to actually liking beer. I ordered it because I have a lot of Irish American history in my family, and I wanted to try it. The name Mooney is a dead giveaway there.

As I took a sip, my brow furrowed, and I looked down at the mug as though seeing it for the first time. This was beer? It was a far cry from the cheap light beer of my earlier experiences. I didn't have to tolerate this. I actually liked it. No—I *really* liked it. I would choose this one again.

That was a huge moment for me.

After trying Guinness, I started searching out good beer. Now I knew it existed. It was harder to find in Georgia than I thought it would be. I found little growler shops and tried new brews, different ones than I had before, at microbreweries. The grocery store started carrying more variety with imports, and local craft brews started invading the shelves too. Like many, I sampled the popular ones, such as Sam Adams.

Now I spend time with my friends in the taproom at the local brewery five minutes from my house.

My story is one of a consumer, but it's not as unique as I thought.

These local brewers, who are passionate about making great beer and seeing the culture of craft brewing spread to local communities around the country, are underdogs in a fight against the big beer companies, which still control a large percentage of the market.

Since craft brewing is a culture with an interesting mix of community and individuality, these breweries understand that they will win the fight one convert at a time.

When the Light Comes On

Craft breweries aren't simply trying to sell product. They want to give people an experience with a beer, to tantalize and excite their taste buds and imaginations with a brew. Brewers love it when they see that happen, especially with people who haven't tried craft beer before.

Bill Butcher from Port City Brewing Company in Alexandria, Virginia, calls it the "light bulb moment." People taste a beer, and it changes their whole perspective about beer. Ask any of his employees, "What was the light bulb moment for you?" They can all tell you.

When Bill was in college, he didn't have much money and bought beer more for quantity than quality for the parties he attended. Every now and then, his dad came to town, took him out, and bought him fancy beer. Good beer.

Bill particularly remembers the Anchor Liberty Ale, a legendary beer in and of itself, as hoppy and unlike anything else he had before. It was so unique. The issue was Anchor's price—too expensive—so it became a special occasion beer. Sierra Nevada's Pale Ale also made an impact on Bill's idea of great beer.

Port City is an interactive place. Groups get a tour of the brewery and sit in the middle of an indoor beer garden at picnic tables, right next to the brewing equipment. It is a great experience.

In these groups, usually one or two people who aren't into beer have come along for the ride with a spouse or friend. This is a challenge. Can Port City convert them?

A common strategy is to get a person to try a flight. Flights are a mainstay at many taprooms—a series of samples placed on a special tray, perhaps made out of wood, to display them well. Whether served to individuals or a group, a flight becomes a way for those new to the brewery to sample the artistry and variety of the beers, to see how they make an IPA or a stout or an ale. With six or eight different choices, customers can pick beers they know they might like, but it also gives them the freedom to get crazy and try something they normally wouldn't.

One of Port City's "beer guides" describes the different flavors, the brewing process, and why the beer tastes the way that it does.

One of Port City's best-selling brews is Optimal Wit, a Belgian-style wit beer. It isn't hoppy, and it's easy to drink—light, citrusy, and refreshing. The beer guides usually start by trying to get people to try that beer.

Often, the moment occurs. Eyes light up. People might say, "I didn't think I liked beer, but I really like this."

Brewers live for that moment.

Hey, If You Like That . . .

In Plainfield, Illinois, forty-five minutes outside of Chicago, Werk Force Brewing Company sees conversions every day. Plainfield is a farming community on the edge of Chicago suburbia. If you go past the city, you'll only see farms.

The normal consumers who walk in for the first time are Busch and Coors Light drinkers. Brandon Wright, the brewer and owner, loves lagers, so they have four or five on tap at a time—a light lager, a pre-Prohibition, an amber lager, and a black pilsner are the standards.

When people come in with buddies and declare that they aren't craft beer fans, Brandon also gives them the light lager, which is so much better than the cheap big-beer products. Most of the time he gets, "This is great!"

Brandon then says, "Hey, if you like that, try this," and suggests other brews. With sample sips, they can try a few before buying. He

Werk Force Sleepy Bear brew.
Courtesy Amanda Wright.

never wants people to buy a beer; sit down; say, "Meh. Not what I like"; and find themselves stuck with a glass of something they don't enjoy. The sampling helps Brandon or another server ask questions, educate, and lead them to one they like.

Then the light bulb comes on.

Werk Force gets a lot of wine drinkers, and they introduce those customers to their line of sours, especially the fruited ones. The customers love them 95 percent of the time.

Most people just haven't found the beer they like yet.

Changing the Definition of Beer

Helping people find a beer they like is giving them a gift, and it's always fun to see someone get a gift.

For Dino Radosta at White Street Brewery in Wake Forest, North Carolina, the brewery taproom is a great place for this type of interaction. People come in with an idea of what beer is, but that is often a narrow view. There is a wide variety of styles and types of beer, and even within those styles, flavors can vary.

The structure of the brewery helps with sampling and experimentation. Why would you walk into a glass blower's shop? To experience that craft and culture. The same thing happens at a brewery, where people can see the big tanks or meet the brewer in an environment different from any other place. The taproom gets people to try new brews and styles and learn the stories behind them.

A brewery can surprise its customers. At a minimum, the staff knows that they like one particular beer and might try others.

When a craft brewery makes a convert—six or seven a week—those become customers for local breweries everywhere.

Spreading the Revolution

Craft breweries are spreading the revolution, but it's how they spread the revolution that's interesting.

Slow Pour Brewing Company is situated outside of the perimeter of Atlanta, Georgia, and the craft revolution has been growing like their name—slowly. It isn't in one of the hipster or cool areas downtown. John Reynolds gets people who like beer, but it's the Bud Light kind, which is understandable. It is common for restaurants in the South to have a Bud Light on its menu.

These customers are perfect for Slow Pour. Just like the brewers already mentioned, John starts them on a blonde ale—his Cotillion Blonde Ale—or the pilsner. Try this, he tells them, and give craft beer a shot.

White Street Kölsch from the tap.
Courtesy White Street Brewing.

An important element for Slow Pour is the power of the community. They try to make a connection with customers individually from the moment they get out of their cars to the time they get back in at the end of the night. Were they served well? Did they have the best experience they could possibly have? Slow Pour pays attention to that.

Liking a new beer is important, but connecting personally with others and making new friends produces a deeper and more meaningful experience.

We Want to Be Your First

When people say they don't like beer, what are they saying? Is it the bitterness they don't enjoy? How hoppy it is?

Revolution Brewing in Chicago doesn't make many crazy or extreme beers. Their forte is making "acceptable" beers. They train their staff to have conversations about beers and make recommendations. Some people know what they like and want; others don't. Helping lead people through the options is part of the service, especially at the Revolution Brewpub.

Revolution wants to be the first craft beer that people taste and like. They know the commonality and the pattern of an individual craft beer conversion, and they love to be part of the story.

Converting fans to craft beer is a continual process. Someone turns twenty-one every day, a potentially new craft lover. When people are young, they drink what is around them, and that is an important time to introduce them to something new and different.

What people want changes all the time. Styles trend up or down, and there are lots of ways to figure out people's preferences. A conversation in a relationship is the best. Revolution has also found that beer fests work well as sampling opportunities.

People used to have no choices. Now there are too many, and all those choices can be daunting, which makes the relationship and education in the local taproom even more important.

Pouring a light lager for a customer at Revolution Brewing.
Courtesy Revolution Brewing.

The taps at Ass Clown Brewery.
Courtesy LunahZon Photography.

A Great Compliment

Matt Glidden of Ass Clown Brewing Company in Cornelius, North Carolina, saw more conversions a few years ago when they began. A big guy once came in dressed in overalls, a cliché country boy, and said not to give him any of that "fruity stuff." After a conversation and a few samples, he walked out with a growler filled with a sour.

Like most brewers, Matt is passionate about his creations. As an artist, he believes that if you'll just try it, you'll find something of his that you'll like. Craft brewers are fighting the bad experiences and cheap standards of a whole industry. Perhaps people just haven't found one they like yet.

When someone does find a beer to enjoy and becomes a fan, that's a great compliment.

Enjoying a flight at Liquid Bread.
Courtesy Liquid Bread.

Get a Flight

Brendan Arnold and Chuck Comeau at Liquid Bread Brewing Co in Hays, Kansas, can tell when customers are from out of town because they order flights of the different flavors to discover which one they like the best. In the end, they might take a couple of growlers or a T-shirt with them. A friend told the brewery they saw a Liquid Bread T-shirt in the Milan airport.

Phil Ferril and Walt Wooden at StillFire Brewery in Suwanee, Georgia, see conversions all the time.

People don't tend to come to a brewery by themselves; they get dragged along with friends. It helps when they have a pathfinder, a friend who has been to the brewery before and knows their friends and what they normally drink, wine or beer or whatever.

Light beer might be the first one people try, but the other extreme can be just as good. The strong flavors in a stout—and adding chocolate or coffee to it—can convert someone just as easily.

Everyday Conversions

Rock Bottom in Nashville, Tennessee, is unique in craft beer because it is part of a restaurant chain. The food in the restaurant is universal in all Rock Bottoms in cities around the country, but the brewery in each is run and operated locally and produces unique recipes by the local brewmaster.

Thomas Mercado is the manager in Nashville, and the Rock Bottom there sits on the busiest street in the city, Broadway. They get new customers all the time from among tourists and others out for a night on the town. The people come from the South and the Midwest, and they are country fans with an almost sacred connection to bad beer.

They come into Rock Bottom and get surprised.

It's a consistent game Thomas plays. Seven out of ten times, when he is talking with customers, they aren't avid craft fans. The rooftop bar boasts twelve taps, and downstairs has sixteen. The barrel-aged

A snifter of stout at StillFire Brewing.
Courtesy Karl Lamb.

Juicy Bits from WeldWerks Brewing.
Courtesy WeldWerks.

products are served downstairs. If Thomas sees people with brown liquor drinks, he strikes up a conversation. They comment that they don't drink beer, only liquor. When he gives them a bourbon barrel-aged beer, they love the flavor. The light comes on.

Now Thomas has turned them on to something new, and they might try other beers, such as a clean Scotch ale.

It's all about surprise and embracing the moment. Thomas has done his job at that point. Being in a tourist area and a chain-type setting, he doesn't know whether they continue drinking craft beer, but he recommends other breweries in town, places run by his friends. He knows the other brewers personally and uses those opportunities to point his customers to them.

A selection of beers from La Cumbre.
Courtesy Cory Campbell.

The Middle of the Journey

Colorado is a different market. WeldWerks Brewing Co isn't a gateway brewery; it's part of a community that has already had some engagement with the craft beer culture.

WeldWerks has big events and tours once a month. They see a few participants from those become new fans. They keep a lager and pilsner on tap for those times, but even their IPAs are approachable and not super bitter. They also have their kettle sours and pastry or dessert stouts. Neil Fisher developed a carrot cake cheesecake IPA. For the customer in the middle of the journey, having those fun, inventive beers can be just as important.

Nerdy about It

Whit Baker at Bond Brothers in Cary, North Carolina, is a nerd about beer and an ally for the conversion.

He didn't really drink before he got into homebrewing. The first thing he did when he started was to try to make better beer. But what is good beer?

Whit read about porters, for example, and then bought five or ten porters, lined them up in shot glasses, and tried to discern the difference and see which ones he liked.

Whit didn't have a single conversion beer; the homebrewing process and hobby converted him to beer.

The new trend is beers that don't taste like beer—heavily fruited kettle sours and pastry stouts are examples. When customers say they don't like beer, modern breweries are less likely to give them a traditional-tasting beer.

Every brewer sees the necessity of converting more people to craft beer. Some people talk about the saturation or the "bubble," but craft beer only has a small percentage of the market dominated by the large beer companies.

Craft brewing still has a long way to go, but it's fought a noble uphill battle to get here.

How did we get here?

THE BEER REVOLUTION

As any brewer will tell you, making beer isn't difficult. Brewing great beer is, but the beverage itself is easy to make.

The Agricultural Revolution allowed humans to stay in one place and populations to grow into cities and beyond. With the abundance of food, despite attempts to store the extra, food spoiled—or fermented.

Fermenting foods weren't necessarily new, but when grains fermented, a new and more nutritious beverage was discovered: beer.

The oldest evidence of beer, from around seven thousand years ago, was found in the area that is now Iran. But the Egyptians made it a part of their everyday lives. The Nile Delta was known as the ancient breadbasket of the world. It's only natural that the Egyptians would develop the beverage that came to be known as liquid bread.

The Egyptians believed that the god Osiris gave them beer, and they used the brew in their religious celebrations. The fermented brews killed the deadly bacteria common in the water of the ancient world. Since beer was safer than water, people drank beer all day, even children as young as two years old—similar to the use of wine in other cultures. Daytime beer had a low alcohol content, tasted sweet, and was filled with nutrients.

They saved the strong beer for special occasions.

Beer was an ingredient in over one hundred medicinal recipes used for general health and healing the sick. The Egyptians paid laborers on large imperial projects with beer. The lower class got the cheap stuff, and royalty enjoyed the high-quality brews. King Tut was buried with a jar of honey beer.[1]

Different regions and cultures developed their own styles and progressed to adding yeast and hops and finding new ways to brew and enjoy the beverage, both for safety and celebration.

This development continued through the centuries. Then a group of upstart European colonies began on the North American continent.

Beer in Early America

Before Europeans arrived, Native Americans made beer from cedar berries, corn, and possibly molasses.

The first English colonists founded the Roanoke colony in 1585, and beer was a mainstay of the diet. Housewives were the first American homebrewers, brewing the drink in their private homes. Taverns served local or country beer with some English imports. Larger cities, such as New York and Philadelphia, distributed down the coast.

Beer wasn't the choice drink for everyone, however. Transportation of beer to rural areas proved difficult, and it often soured. Farmers discovered that it was easier to turn grain into whiskey, which took up less room and kept better. They could also carry whiskey in a flask.[2]

The philosophy of moderation dominated colonial life; alcohol was fine if it didn't interfere with worship and work.

As the country grew west, pioneers and hardworking Americans couldn't waste time with barley or hops. Cider and brandy proved easier to produce, and rum was cheap.[3]

The attitude toward alcohol began to change. Instead of drinking in moderation, Americans drank to get the buzz, with little thought of social pleasure or community, which created trouble. With the early Puritan religious influence, people in the US no longer saw alcohol as a necessity but as a problem.

In this context, immigration boomed in the 1800s. Six hundred thousand immigrants arrived in the US in the 1830s, 1.7 million in the 1840s, and 2.6 million in the 1850s. Three-quarters of those immigrants were from Germany and Ireland—beer drinkers.

The American Beverage

The Irish had a drinking culture, but they had fled a potato famine and abject poverty. They were just trying to survive.

The Germans left their country due to riots, famine, land disputes, and political oppression. Young men looking for the promise of economic freedom and opportunity left for America. These were independent-minded entrepreneurs. While the Irish stayed on the east coast, many Germans made their way to the Midwest, bringing their culture and brewing craft with them.[4]

Small breweries dotted the landscape of America in the mid-1800s. In many small towns, a brewery, often built in residential locations, was the first business. Most of those early German breweries lasted no more than five years, but a select few survived.

English ale had never been as popular as cider and spirits in the United States. German immigrants introduced the lager, light in body and color and lower in alcohol content. The rising German population and curious American drinkers, ready for something lighter, created high demand.

Most breweries didn't survive because the small populations of smaller cities and towns limited the customer base. For Pabst, Miller, Blatz, and others, the smaller communities in the Midwest meant they needed to expand their distribution. They had to think on a national scale and invest in long-distance shipping to survive.[5]

For men such as Philip Best and Joseph Schlitz, the quality of the beer was paramount. They were creative thinkers who were willing to adapt and use new technology, such as railroads and refrigeration. Beer soon became the most popular American beverage through the late nineteenth century.

The German brewers re-created their culture of social connection and community around great beer and adapted it for America, whose citizens latched onto the lager as a drink for communal events, a compromise between the extremities of gluttonous drinking and the growing Temperance movement. The German culture flew in the face of the Temperance message. It was a culture that stood as proof that it was possible to combine drinking alcohol with respectability, industry, pleasure, and decency.[6]

One of the American adaptations of the German culture was the competitive nature and big business of the beer industry. The bigger brewers began to crush the smaller ones.

At the same time, the German and Irish drinking culture clashed with the American hatred of alcohol. In addition, anti-immigrant feelings, the fight with Germany in World War I, and legitimate problems with some American saloons that used illegal activities (gambling, prostitution, etc.) to stay in business (under the thumb of the massive big brewers) led to increased support for the Temperance movement in the US.

Prohibition passed with an amendment to the Constitution in 1919.

Prohibition

Most US breweries were owned by second- and third-generation German families, with German names on the bottles, and they made perfect targets during World War I. These companies were owned by the "enemy." Lack of support for Prohibition became unpatriotic. The propaganda stated that those who cared about America wanted to destroy alcohol.[7]

Temperance was the social reform movement of its day, popular with politicians and religious leaders.

Prohibition—meant to make the nation safer; stop drunk, abusive husbands; and improve working-class life—did the opposite. It demonized German and Irish immigrants, and the end of the corporate legal structure opened opportunities for criminal organizations to take over and get rich on the black market.

These new gangs (the Mafia) bribed politicians and became territorial, leading to violence. The most famous act of violence was the St. Valentine's Massacre in 1929, where a few of Al Capone's men, dressed as police officers, gunned down seven men from a rival gang in Chicago.[8]

Homebrewing became popular again during Prohibition.

Thousands of local and regional breweries closed during the years of Prohibition. The large ones survived by switching to sodas, cheese, or other products. When Prohibition ended, strong ones that survived were ready to take over the market.

Consolidation

Unfortunately, when Prohibition ended in 1933, the United States was mired in the worst economic crisis in its history. Politicians might have hoped that legalizing alcohol would help the economy, but years of Prohibition meant that American tastes had changed to sodas and whiskey (which were easier to make in secret at home). With mobsters unwilling to let go of their profits without a fight, only the bigger beer companies could make it through the years that followed.[9]

Once the Depression ended, other realities impacted the brewing industry. Before Prohibition, 90 percent of beer was on tap. With bottles, the revolutionary aluminum can, and refrigerators in every home, 80 percent of consumers drank their beer at home by 1960. The goal was no longer great beer but mass-produced beer that could be distributed around the country. Success became dependent on marketing through radios and televisions, which were also invading every home.[10]

Local neighborhood breweries were all but gone. Americans came to care about quantity, not quality. TV dinners, sweetened cereals, and cheap beer ruled the day for a generation or more.

When some Americans, especially young people disillusioned by the Vietnam War, racism, and political corruption, began to revolt against the status quo, a few fringe men and women sought quality and community again.

Craft beer was born.

The Spark in California

The late 1960s saw a rebellion against the shrink-wrapped, stale consumer culture in America. California pioneered that counterculture, and it became the perfect place and time to explore a different kind of brewery. It started small. Most people hardly noticed.

A twenty-five-year-old beer lover came to California in 1965. Fritz Maytag, from the family that made washing machines, sat in a local pub and drank his favorite beer from a local brewery, Anchor. The bartender told him to enjoy it since it might be his last. Anchor made sour beer that was notoriously bad, but Maytag saw an opportunity.

He bought controlling interest in the brewery in 1967. Soon, he brewed artful, tasty beers. The brewery grew in business and popularity through California, eventually distributing across the country. Anchor was the first independent "craft" brewery in the United States.

The state also boasted the first brewing program in the country at the University of California, Davis, in 1958. It became a hallmark of homebrewing and new brewers trying to learn about and start small breweries.

Jack McAuliffe had visited Scotland and acquired a taste for English ales. After stopping by Anchor Brewing for some inspiration, he built his own brewery in Sonoma, California, in 1977. It's regarded as the first modern microbrewery in the United States. McAuliffe named his brewery New Albion in honor of pre-Prohibition Albion Ale and Porter Brewing in San Francisco. New Albion later closed, but it influenced many in the region and across the country.[11]

The Bible of Homebrewing

If you wanted great, or even good, beer in the seventies, you had to brew it at home. Homebrewing was illegal, but the law wasn't enforced, so those looking for something palatable to drink took up the hobby.

Charlie Papazian attended the University of Virginia, but he didn't drink beer because the stuff he had didn't taste very good. A neighbor introduced him to homebrewing, and then he and friends concocted their first brews in the basement of a day care center, after hours. Papazian was hooked.

After graduating with a degree in nuclear engineering in 1972, he moved to Boulder, Colorado, with his friend. He got a teaching position at a local school and homebrewed in the evenings. His friends caught word of his hobby, and he started teaching others.

It was "outlaw brewing," and the people who practiced it were out-of-the-box pioneers. All they had were limited malts and simple methods, but compared to the cheap, mass-produced beer of the time, their brew tasted great. If not for homebrewing, Papazian wouldn't have started drinking beer at all. He wrote a book, *The Complete Joy of Homebrewing*, that was ultimately called the "brewing bible." He started the association of brewers that later merged with another organization to become the American Brewers Association.[12]

Homebrewing became legal in 1978, and, in the years to come, Papazian helped lay the foundation of a craft beer culture of collaboration and cooperation with the Great American Beer Fest that started in the early eighties. It was held in Boulder the first year, but then it moved to Denver, where thousands attend every year.

From the Old Country

Charles Finkel loved the great beer from Europe and began importing it from Germany, the UK, and Belgium, exposing the locals in Seattle, Washington, to different styles and more complex flavors. Finkel opened Pike Brewing Company in 1989 and was best known for the XXXXX Stout, a nod to English roots. While it wasn't the first brewery in Seattle, he had an important impact on the next generation of brewers through the introduction of those European imports.[13]

Bert Grant was born in Dundee, Scotland; grew up in Toronto, Canada; and settled in Yakima, Washington. He flaunted his Scottish roots and donned a kilt whenever he could. He brewed his ale for his own pleasure, and he made that clear.

When he was younger, Grant started testing and tasting beer at a Toronto Brewery. When thirty years in US corporate beer wore on him, Grant moved to Yakima, with Washington State hops all around him. He tinkered with recipes until he made "the Ale Master"—the perfect ale. Friends agreed and helped him open a brewery.

In July 1981, the state raised the limit to 8 percent alcohol by volume (ABV). Two weeks later, now with the freedom to brew other recipes with higher ABV, Grant's Scottish ale went out to local saloons. Grant continued to experiment with styles and opened the first brewpub in Washington since before Prohibition. He put the pub in an old railway station and held court at a table in the middle of the room well into his seventies. He died in 2001, and the pub closed soon after.

Grant was a legend in the craft industry and has been credited with establishing the Northwest style of hoppier India pale ale.[14]

The Legend Continues

Other notable figures have risen to change the face of craft beer since the 1980s. The breweries run by people such as Jim Koch (Sam Adams) and Ken Grossman (Sierra Nevada) began to grow and took the alternative to Big Beer to the national level. While many may argue that these are no longer "craft beers," they influenced beer drinkers and brewers across the country to create independent, delicious, quality beverages.

That dream is still at the heart of the craft movement, which is fueled by stories of individuals with dreams of making great beer, making their marks, connecting to the community and history, and continuing the revolution on their own terms.

Every brewer has a story of their own.

THE PASSION AND THE DREAM

Local breweries are rich with stories. Every conversion, every brewer, every beer, and every brewery has its own history.

The people who invested their lives in the craft industry have character and resiliency. They are Davids, willing to stand up to Goliath with nothing but a few little stones. They are dreamers, philosophers, and believers in the culture.

My personal introduction to brewing came from friends who homebrewed. Before that, I enjoyed great beer from local growler shops and the occasional set of cans or bottles from the grocery store.

A homebrewing friend would hear that I liked good beer—specifically craft beer—and would invite me over to drink their concoctions, usually made five gallons at a time. I gladly sampled the different brews and became educated in the process as the creators gushed about their recipes and asked for feedback.

Several of them expressed the same dream. They wanted to start their own breweries, each with its own story and unique spin on the common passion for great beer and community.

The laws in Georgia changed recently to allow retail and distribution for the brewer, and more local breweries opened up, including those of a few of my friends.

As you'll see with the sampling of stories that follow, each brewer has worked to bring something of value to the community and the world through great beer. From the chain restaurant extreme of Rock Bottom to the über local and individual mentality of Ass Clown, each took a different path but arrived with the same purpose: to change the way people think about beer.

Bill Butcher of Port City Brewing Company
(Alexandria, DC)

Bill Butcher began in the wine business. He always enjoyed quality beer and joked that after tasting wine all day, he liked nothing better than to have a nice cold beer when he got home to cleanse the palate.

Now that he tastes beer all day, he pours a glass of wine when he gets home.

His background is in sales, distributing, and marketing—specifically brand building. More than ten years ago, he and his wife, Karen, wanted to support the local agricultural community and producers. They found that all the craft beer they enjoyed drinking came from the West Coast. Beer consists of mostly water, so importing it from so far away was not the most environmentally sound way to do it. Why were they shipping water?

The Butchers wondered whether they could find local or East Coast beer like the ones they imported from the West Coast. They explored local options in 2008, but they couldn't find a beer that was similar to the one they loved, the Sierra Nevada Pale Ale. They appreciated the hoppiness, color, aroma, and delicious taste. They sought to match the standard.

Metro Washington, DC, was the only top twenty-five city (by population) in the US that didn't have a packaging brewery. What if the Butchers could brew and distribute high-quality beer? Maybe people would give them a shot.

The Butchers incorporated Port City in 2009 and opened in 2011 as the first modern packaging brewery in the District of Columbia.

There was a great brew pub and beer culture at the time, and the Butchers wanted to get into the market and build a great brand like those of the famous West Coast–style beers—only from the East Coast, something that was missing in the market.

At first, the Butchers researched why others hadn't done this before. They couldn't find a reason. It wasn't that others had tried and failed. It was just something that was missing from the market. All they needed was high-quality beer, and people would give them the chance.

Bill Butcher from Port City.
Courtesy Port City Brewing.

Their vision was to be the best local brewery in the area. DC is an international market. People visit from around the world, and beers are imported from other countries. It also has some of the greatest restaurants in the country. In this sophisticated environment, the Butchers' vision was to brew a beer that would be not only the best in the area but also compete with others from around the world.

Port City emulates wine tourism with hospitality and education in a craft setting. It has a tasting room and educational pours, much as the wine business does in Napa Valley.

Brandon Wright of Werk Force Brewing Company
(Plainfield, Illinois)

As a college student in 2003, Brandon Wright fell in love with home-brewing on his kitchen stove. He majored in university studies at Southern Illinois University and brewed every day. From the stovetop, he graduated to a turkey fryer on the front porch and evolved to teaching other college students how to homebrew.

He grabbed every book he could and read every online article on the topic, and he joined the American Homebrewers Association and a local homebrew club when he moved to the suburbs of Chicago in 2005. There was no doubt that he wanted to open a brewery one day, but he had no money. No professional experience.

Brandon floated around to odd jobs, all the while contacting and walking into every brewery in Chicago to try to get into the business. A couple of offers came his way, but they never felt right.

In the meantime, he worked a corporate job at Office Max and hated it. When an opportunity at a winery opened, he jumped at it and worked there for a year, adding a great deal to his homebrewing experience—fermentation, racking, barreling techniques, and bottling. Fall turned to winter, and the winery laid everyone off. Brandon went back to the cubicle life.

This time, he worked in corporate real estate and high-level transactions. Then the recession hit.

Brandon's wife, Amanda, was an entrepreneur, a photographer with her own company, so after some time in real estate, he knew it was time to go for it.

His first idea was to open Brandon's House of Awesomeness, which would carry items from all his interests—skateboards, fishing tackle, homebrewing supplies, and more. Amanda nixed the idea. Since he loved homebrewing, he chose that. He found a small storefront and signed a lease. With the little bit of leftover money, he purchased a pallet of supplies, a computer, and point-of-sale service.

He incorporated the business in 2011 and opened in January 2012. The local homebrew club—Plainfield Ale and Lager Enthusiasts (PALE)—supported Brandon and gave him instant business. He made no money for three years and wondered when he would ever get a paycheck.

One year in, the county served him with a letter stating that he wasn't authorized to sell homebrew equipment and supplies. He was in unincorporated real estate, with the incorporated area literally across the street. Confused, he called the county, thinking they had the wrong person, but they confirmed that he wasn't properly zoned and had to pay $500 a day, retroactively from when he opened.

He could have quit, with too much to overcome, but he had passion and a dream and felt ownership in it. He knew the county didn't understand what the homebrew store was about.

Brandon hired an attorney, a stereotypical crotchety old man from Joliette who smoked cigars. The attorney, angry at the county because he thought it was screwing the homebrew store, helped for free.

Going into the hearing, Brandon was nervous. The head of every department in the county sat around a big U-shaped table.

At the end of the hearing, the county allowed him to sell online, but he had to sign a document that he would treat the retail store like a pharmacy—people had to walk in, sit at a computer, and order online. Then he could hand the product over the counter. After five months of that, he informed the county that he couldn't do it anymore. His business was dying.

The situation became more complicated when the owner lost the building, and the bank took ownership of Brandon's lease. When the bank wouldn't let him out of the lease, he would have been lost without his background in real estate. He found the clause in the lease that specified the retail allowance and explained the county's position.

The bank let him out of the lease.

Hope arrived when the nearby incorporated area of Plainfield contacted him to ask him to move his business into the Village of Plainfield. The village gave him a special permit and welcomed him with open arms.

By 2013, the homebrew shop had purchased some equipment and started making money. He decided that it was time to live his dream of opening a brewery. The government shutdown in October delayed the process, but Brandon got all the permits he needed to open Werk Force in May 2014, and he connected the brewery to the homebrew shop.

Brandon was the sole brewer of a two-barrel brewhouse. He started in 2014 with four taps and brewed nonstop. Werk Force grew to eight taps, and then twelve. Now they brew 550 barrels a year in that two-barrel house.

Insane, but that's what a dream will do.

Scott Wood of the Courtyard Brewery (New Orleans, Louisiana)

In 2001, several breweries existed, but there wasn't wide recognition that they were part of the fabric of the local neighborhood.

Beer dominated Scott Wood's personal history. One of his great grandfathers owned a brewery in Montana before Prohibition. Someone from every generation since was in production, sales, or even bootlegging.

Prohibition was tragic from a community standpoint. New Orleans is known for its old buildings and ghost stories—but also for alcohol consumption, another definition of *spirits*. After Prohibition, they lost the community aspect with the conglomeration of beer, a departure from the original experience of breweries. With local breweries, people naturally gravitate back to being in a community.

Scott's beer background was on the distribution side. He left the beer industry three times, but it always pulled him back in.

Scott married a woman from New Orleans and moved there from San Diego in 2009. Noticing a dearth of breweries, and none like the ones he enjoyed in San Diego, he was inspired to open one.

Louisiana and New Orleans were still dealing with the fallout from Prohibition, in that some of the laws and ideas had never been challenged in the South and still hindered growth.

He got into homebrewing to make the beers, such as the IPAs, that he missed from San Diego. At the time, no one crafted those in New Orleans. It was a hobby, but the more he brewed, the better he got. Scott brewed so much beer in his home that he couldn't hold enough parties to get rid of it all. Once he got through the legal hurdles, he could make money from it. Scott's brother, wanting to own something in the beer industry, fed him the story that beer was in the family's blood.

Scott's creativity and enthusiasm for brewing came from his home-brewing experience. Everyone he looks up to in the industry or believes is a notable figure started in homebrewing. Even those who went to brew school started as homebrewers.

He took his passion for great beer and opened the Courtyard in New Orleans with his brother's support.

Dino Radosta of White Street Brewing Company (Wake Forest, North Carolina)

Some people get to craft brewing from a different path.

Dino Radosta retired in his early forties after selling his software business. He was originally from New Orleans, so he had grown up in a city with a subculture organized by enclaves and neighborhoods.

Dino moved to North Carolina in 1997, where the closest town was Wake Forest. Like many small towns, Wake Forest enjoyed its heyday in the twenties or thirties. Hard times arrived in the 1970s, and people left the center of town, leaving behind older, well-crafted structures that no longer had purpose. The vibrancy was gone.

Memories and stories connect us to the past and survive beyond us, but often it's what we see, the buildings, that connects us. Old buildings inspire imagination and questions about the people who came before and what they were doing.

In downtown Wake Forest, older buildings were abandoned or modernized. Dino wondered who the modernization was supposed to appeal to, and it pissed him off to see these great elements of history being torn down to put up condos. Their history would be forgotten within ten years.

Dino decided to do something about it. He started buying old buildings and restored them to their original character. Then he leased them.

There was one old, decrepit building that was so awful, he wondered why he had bought it. It was in such bad shape, he didn't have

The bar and taps at White Street Brewing.
Courtesy White Street Brewing.

a vision for it. What could it be? What should it be? They didn't need another nail salon. He wanted it to be a business that could revitalize the downtown.

He wanted to create a place to make new friends and talk with old ones—a place where people would say, "This is my spot." They would know the people and have a history there. He pondered what could do that—perhaps a movie theater, night club, or art museum? Restaurants were everywhere and failed all the time. The business would have to do something to set it apart. Maybe it would brew its own beer.

Dino researched what it took to brew beer. He decided that he didn't even need a restaurant. Breweries were once social houses where people went to talk and be with their neighbors.

That was the answer.

In 2011, Dino had no idea that a craft revolution was happening. He didn't even drink beer or know how to make it. His motivation was simply to bring people downtown.

But his love and appreciation for the old buildings connected with the craft revolution. Find a library that was built in 1930 and compare it with one built today. Both have the same purpose, but the character and craftsmanship are vastly different. Back in the thirties, erecting a civic building involved a sense of pride and permanence in the community. Many local businesses were owned by "moms and pops" who invested their life savings in a permanent structure, permeated with care and individuality. They wanted it to last.

He discovered that craft brewing had many of the same principles— a throwback to a simpler time and history, a change of culture, a rebellion against the shrink-wrapped and branded consumer culture, and the importance of community and the local neighborhood. Craft brewers take their time and invest in something so that they can say, "My name is on this," and give people products they can be proud of.

Dino couldn't brew beer, so he found someone who could make fantastic, approachable beer. He didn't want it to draw beer nerds, but he needed the highest quality. White Street opened (on White Street) and started winning awards. Their Kolsch style is a best seller and won the gold medal in the World Beer Cup.

Jeff Erway of La Cumbre Brewing Company (Albuquerque, New Mexico)

Sometimes you get lucky when you have nothing else to do.

Jeff Erway could play most instruments passably. He got a job as a music teacher out on a Navajo reservation. Out in the middle of nowhere, there was nothing for him and his wife to spend money or time on. So he homebrewed and poured what little money they had on supplies and spent his extensive free time concocting brews.

A year later, five people from Teach for America moved next door. Every night after school became happy hour at Jeff's place. Soon, he brewed twice a week for seven to fifteen people. The only way to get good at brewing is to do it for twenty to thirty hours a week, so brewing became a part-time job for him.

Jeff was always obsessed with something. When he was five to eight years old, it was LEGO. At twelve to thirteen, it was guitar. Kurt

Jeff Erway of La Cumbre.
Courtesy Cory Campbell.

Cobain died, and Jeff immersed himself in grunge music. In college, it was cars.

By the time he was twenty-two, he was already passionate about craft beer. He loved the comradery of the industry and how friendly the people he met were. The only competition among them was about who made the better beer. Most brewers were trying to contribute to growth of the whole industry, not trying to take business away from anyone else. That inspired him.

With a passion for great beer and hundreds of hours of practice, Jeff decided to pursue brewing professionally. He left teaching in 2007, and, after graduating from the American Brewers Guild, he took a position as an assistant brewer in Albuquerque, New Mexico. A veteran brewer continued to teach him brewing skills and techniques, which took him from a homebrewer to commercial success.

That veteran brewer already had plans to open his own brewery with some partners, and Jeff became the de facto head brewer when the vet left.

After two years as the head brewer, he felt that to continue to grow in the industry, he needed to open his own brewery. He opened La Cumbre in 2010. The brewery grew to forty-nine employees by the end of 2019 but has cut back to forty-five in 2020. When they started, Jeff was the only brewer. Now he's only in the brewhouse once a month and spends most of his time running the business, sharing ownership with his wife and other investors.

John Reynolds of Slow Pour Brewing Company (Lawrenceville, Georgia)

John Reynolds graduated from the University of Georgia and started working in information technology. The IT industry was very cut and dry—a corporate life with little room for creativity.

John had always been a craft beer nerd but had never brewed it before. He had always hesitated to put that much energy in a hobby, worried that it would start to be like work. But then the luck of the draw changed that.

Because his wife's family is so large, they draw names for gifts at Christmas. When John drew his brother-in-law's name one year, he bought him a long-coveted old-style Coke bottle machine.

The next year, that same brother-in-law drew John's name and gave him a homebrew kit.

John started brewing. He went all grain on the first batch and scorched it. The brew tasted terrible, but he fell in love with the brewing and the whole process. Homebrewing allowed him a creative outlet outside of technology and the corporate lifestyle. No one could tell him what he could or couldn't do with it.

He came home from work and set up in the front yard. The anticipation and excitement grew as he waited to see what each batch would be like. The science interested him, but with homebrewing, he was limited by what changes he could make.

Five years passed, and his brother-in-law opened a coffee shop in the area. John suggested that his brother-in-law partner with an up-and-coming brewer and provide coffee for a stout. The brother-in-law had another idea. What if they started their own brewery?

A band plays in the evening at Slow Pour.
Courtesy Slow Pour.

John didn't take the idea seriously at first. Unlike many homebrewers, he wasn't open with his beer and didn't want people judging what he brewed. He brewed ten gallons, put it in kegs on his kegerator at home, and he and his wife, Iara, consumed it over time. He was shy about it because the brewing felt very personal to him. He didn't want people telling him that his "kids" were ugly.

The local community helped to inspire him, however. John and his wife grew up around Lawrenceville, Georgia. Gwinnett County, Georgia had been a black hole for craft beer since Prohibition. For years, the Reynoldses went to Lawrenceville on a date once a week or so. Atlanta and Athens were forty-five minutes away, but Lawrenceville was closer and had nice downtown square with eclectic restaurants.

The older buildings were being restored and rebuilt, returning much of the history to the downtown area. The town was coming back to life.

It needed something else, however—something that would make it a full night for people who wanted to walk around and hang out.

Lawrenceville needed a brewery. After more than a decade in the IT industry and with his brother-in-law as a partner, John decided to start one.

They found and purchased a building quickly, but the next part of the process took two and a half years—obtaining permits and hiring lawyers to get city council on board. Laws had to be rewritten or changed. Provisions and legal considerations had to be worked through the city to allow them to brew and serve.

John still worked in IT while he was planning the brewery and buying the building. He wondered when he would leave his job, and what the transition would look like.

Every year around the holidays, the company he worked for had sizeable layoffs. The same pattern happened in 2016. He went to lunch one day, sat in the parking lot, and thought that he would be excited if he was laid off. He was probably one of the few who thought that.

He returned from lunch, and the company invited him on a phone call with two hundred other people, and they laid him off. He couldn't wait to leave work.

John has two passions. One is beer. The other is tattoos. That afternoon, he left his job and got a tattoo.

The severance helped with his finances and gave him some time, but the brewery wasn't in a position to pay him yet. John took a holdover position at a friend's marketing tech company.

As time passed, John wanted out of the corporate job, hoping for his brother-in-law to have everything ready. John's heart wasn't in the nine-to-five, making it difficult to stay. He stayed at that company for seven months.

The partners knew they couldn't go from front yard homebrewing to commercial brewing without help. Wanting to come to the market with products they were proud of, they hired a friend from another Georgia brewery to mentor and consult for them for a year before they opened, and the professional brewer expedited the process.

John wasn't going to dip his toe into the brewery or do it halfway. He would either commit to it or not. To him, that would determine the type of company they would be. Three months before they opened, John quit his job and started brewing.

It was surreal. In 2017, Slow Pour was the first craft brewery in the county since Prohibition. John is proud to have been a part of that.

In the beginning, it was just John and the consultant in the brew room. John ran the brewing and the tasting room. It led to long days, 7:00 a.m. to midnight every day.

As the brewery grew, the partners' first present to themselves was hiring a tasting room manager, another of John's brothers-in-law. That manager has since left to start his own business, but now, with a new manager and three brewers, John has stepped away from brewing to run the business.

Josh Deth of Revolution Brewing
(Chicago, Illinois)

Josh Deth always wanted to figure out how things worked and do them himself. He got into craft brewing and homebrewing in college. Fortunately, he lived in a co-op house with other people and a big kitchen, complete with a stove and equipment on hand to brew—and people to drink the beer.

Homebrewing is a supportive community, and Josh networked with others. He took a class on brewing and became best friends with the teacher. Like others, he found that homebrewing was a great way to build a community and a gateway to start working at a brewery.

During the summer of 1995, he caught a lucky break when he got a job at Golden Prairie, a small but pioneering brewery in Chicago. He assisted the brewer and cleaned kegs part time. Later, he changed jobs and began at the bottom rung of the ladder at Goose Island, also in Chicago. However, his ultimate dream was to start his own brewery.

But in the mid-1990s, Chicago had a spotty record with breweries. Josh opened a restaurant and bar first, in 2003. At the time, it seemed more feasible than opening a brewery.

He wanted to do something that would encourage business for the community, as he lived in the neighborhood. He found a building in

Pallets and logos at Revolution.
Courtesy Revolution Brewing.

2007 and spent three years developing it and putting a brewhouse in the back.

Revolution Brewing opened in 2010. It began as a brew pub and has grown into a regional production.

There weren't many breweries in Chicago when Revolution opened. By 2019, there were around one hundred in the city, with twelve open or about to open within a mile of Revolution. It was exciting for Josh to be part of pioneering something new.

Matt Glidden of Ass Clown Brewing Company (Cornelius, North Carolina)

Mortgages provided a good living. Matt Glidden worked for a few companies and lived comfortably as a mortgage broker, but he didn't love it.

Taproom and bar at Ass Clown.
Courtesy LunahZon Photography.

He had a passion for working with his hands and experiencing the art behind creating or building something. Beer kits gave him the perfect opportunity to work on that passion, and he tweaked the recipes.

In the early 2000s, Matt considered New Castle, Guinness, and Blue Moon examples of craft beer. He attended beer fests and developed his knowledge of styles and the craft industry. The name "Ass Clown" originated during his time in mortgages, a ribbing type of joke among close friends. At the same time, Matt was exploring beer fests that weren't as evolved as they are today—no water, no food. And his own behavior after hundreds of samples of high ABV beer helped the name to stick.

Loving beer was one thing, but he wasn't sure he could make a living at it. He took a step forward in 2009. He put up a wall at his mortgage office, brought in his homebrew system and glass jars, and opened a little shop. He joked with his customers that they would grab a beer and sign mortgage papers. They never did that, of course.

Matt had no investors or money, but with his passion for creating great beer, he moved forward, doing all the work himself. It was difficult. Now he sees why people bring in other owners or investors. It would have been nice to have people to do marketing or bookkeeping or manage the taproom. It was a struggle to be everywhere at once, and he got stretched thin and stressed.

He got his license in April 2011 and opened the second-oldest brewery in Charlotte. It was very small at the time.

Since Matt wanted a name that stuck out and piqued curiosity, calling the brewery Ass Clown seemed like the perfect fit.

The city didn't know what to do with him or what to expect. His business didn't fit the existing categories. A brewery isn't a bar or a restaurant. It's not an event hall, but it creates community and holds events.

Ass Clown grew, other craft breweries opened, and the tax dollars came in. The city began to understand and appreciate what the breweries brought to the community. People traveled to Charlotte just to visit the brewery. In 2019, more than 80 percent of Ass Clown's customers came from out of state.

The name causes tension in the Bible Belt, but there's power in the name too. Matt doesn't spend a dime on advertising. New customers find out about the brewery by word of mouth. With the slow build in demand, Ass Clown has grown to a ten-gallon brewhouse.

Brendan Arnold and Chuck Comeau of Liquid Bread Brewing Co (Hays, Kansas)

Building the local community is the goal for Brendan Arnold and Chuck Comeau. The beer they produce is for the customers they see every day, not for the people in the next town over.

Prohibition still had an impact on beer in Kansas, even into the twenty-first century, as it did in many states. The old laws were designed for wineries and other industries, not the unique craft beer

Outside Liquid Bread at night.
Courtesy Liquid Bread Brewing.

market. Kansas has a great community of craft breweries, and the Craft Brewers Guild focuses on the needs of the local brewers.

When Brendan and Chuck started talking about doing something unique in terms of food and beer in Hays, they gravitated toward working with a talented brewmaster who presented flavors that were different from what most people expected. Combining great food and beer appealed to them. They decided to start a microbrewery and restaurant.

They opened at a time when the craft industry started taking off, along with a growing sense of conscientious consumerism, and it was like a tsunami for them. They rode that wave way ahead of anyone else when they opened Liquid Bread (also known as Lb) Brewing in 2003.

Brendan had done a little homebrewing in college, and he managed bars and coffee shops for years in Hays. While managing one of those restaurants, he attended brewing school at the legendary Seibel Institute. He wanted to learn to make high-quality products without the trial and error of homebrewing. The modern access to classes and schools helped Brendan make great strides in brewing amazing beer.

After taking classes in Chicago and Munich, Brendan was almost finished with an advanced brewing theory certificate in 2019.

Shaun Yasaki of Noble Beast Brewing Company (Cleveland, Ohio)

Opening his own brewery was never Shaun Yasaki's goal.

He started homebrewing, but he only made twelve or so batches. His first job in a brewery was at a local establishment. Brewing great beer was the goal, but as he learned more about the industry and community, a wild thought entered his mind. Maybe he could open his own place one day.

Shaun later worked at another brewery, where he learned all the different aspects of brewing great beer, a little of everything.

After gaining all that experience, he left the brewpub to help someone start another brewery. He was the brewmaster and co-owner, and

Outside Noble Beast at night.
Courtesy Shaun Yasaki.

he picked up the skills to build out and manage a brewery. After two years, he decided to leave and start his own brewery in 2017.

The only thing he didn't have experience in was getting financing and creating a business on his own. It was a huge learning curve for him, but Noble Beast was born and started to thrive.

Phil Ferril and Walt Wooden of StillFire Brewery (Suwanee, Georgia)

A friend and elder at the Presbyterian church got into craft brewing and helped Walt Wooden start making beer at home by taking him to the brew store for ingredients. Back in the late '90s, the internet didn't offer the same options, and it was difficult to get things shipped. People needed the local homebrew store.

Patio area of StillFire Brewing.
Courtesy Karl Lamb.

Walt's goal was to make beer cheaper than he could buy Bud Light at the store. It wasn't always better.

Walt's brother also got into homebrewing, and eventually they made some great beer.

It was a long learning process. Practice made them better, and the technology also improved. When the internet came along, Walt could find more answers about how to fix problems. With some research, he could find people on the internet who knew more than he did, and he could order anything he wanted and have it shipped in two days.

Phil Ferril was always interested in both beer and the brewing process. His father and uncle in New York owned a pub. The beer menu—eight different beers—was amazing for the time. They had a stout, an amber, and other imports.

In the 1970s, the air force sent Phil overseas, which allowed him to try beers he had only heard about. They tasted different in Europe, and those beers piqued his interest.

Back then, it was illegal to homebrew, a law that dated back to after Prohibition when alcohol was legalized again. The large brewers had asked for laws that protected their businesses from competition so that they could grow. Laws against homebrewing were part of those.

In 1900, there were over three thousand breweries in the US. People made their own beer everywhere, and there was variety. By the 1970s, the number of breweries nationwide went down to one hundred.

Being in the air force, Phil wouldn't do anything illegal. President Jimmy Carter legalized homebrewing in 1978, but between family and deployments, Phil didn't have time to homebrew, even with his interest and passion for great beer (which included picking up pamphlets and looking up books in the library). He was even in Colorado Springs during the 1970s when Charlie Papazian was below the radar and homebrewing.

It took moving to Georgia in 1993 and brewing with a friend to get Phil into homebrewing. He went to a local homebrew shop and received a great deal of "take this kit and add this packet of grain" kind of advice from others who were already homebrewing.

He joined the Brews Brothers, a local homebrewing club, and, when they dissolved, the core of that group started the Brewmasters of Alpharetta, which eventually started the homebrew contest at the Suwanee Beer Fest.

When he could—more consistently in the late 1990s and early 2000s—Phil went to beer festivals, such as the Great American Beer Fest and the Oregon Brewers Festival. Since 2002, he's attended every Homebrew Conference, now called Homebrew Con.

In the beginning, homebrewing was fairly primitive—valves, hoses, and ice chests. People didn't have pumps so they used gravity, which could be depended on, instead of electricity. Simple was better. Adding pumps and newer equipment makes the system more expensive and complicated, and more can break.

There were some brewpubs in 1994, but the 6 percent alcohol cap cut out some styles and imports, limiting those who wanted to innovate and create.

Through the Suwanee Beer Fest, Phil met Randall Veugeler, who had also done some homebrewing and loved craft beer. Randall and his wife, Angie, started the Suwanee Beer Fest, and Phil judged the best in show at the homebrew contest.

Time passed, and one day Randall asked if Phil had ever wanted to brew commercially. Of course, Phil had considered it but didn't think it was an option anymore. Randall told Phil about talks with the city of Suwanee to put a brewery in the old fire station.

It was a great location. Phil was in.

Walt Wooden had worked for Randall for nine years, building websites at the Veugeler Design Group. When he was first hired, Walt noticed a wall of about two hundred beer bottles housed on special shelves and realized that Randall was into beer, so he brought his homebrew kit to the office. They decided to set up a brew system at the office with an expensive electric system. Walt would brew on Saturdays.

Walt and Phil met at the Suwanee Beer Fest and at competitions. Together with other investors and owners, they started the brewery in the old fire station, StillFire Brewery, in 2019.

Thomas Mercado of Rock Bottom (Nashville, Tennessee)

Thomas Mercado got his first break in the craft industry while traveling abroad. Four Pines Brewing company gave him an internship, and he and his wife moved to Australia for a year.

Thomas started homebrewing in college. His wife was a pastry chef and showed him how to make things from scratch. He was surprised by how much he enjoyed cooking and creating different foods. Hot dogs had been a staple of his diet, so both the craft and the better-tasting food impressed and mystified him.

That idea transferred to beer. He loved beer and heard that people made their own. The process sparked his interest and creativity, and it was more economical than buying beer at the bars. He brought bottles of his own brew in his backpack and opened them in the alleyways behind bars to join the party scene without spending a lot of money.

Moving out to Australia with his wife in 2011 was a "flag in the ground" moment for him to commit to craft beer and nothing else. "From this moment," he thought, "I'll do nothing but craft beer." In Sydney, he started bartending and cold-calling breweries.

It wasn't until he started working at Four Pines that he realized that people made careers out of beer—and not just selling or branding it. Brewing beer for a living sounded like a phenomenal job.

He had to take it seriously though, saying no to the other jobs he'd had before. He couldn't settle.

Because the Australian scene was smaller than California's, it was easier to get experience and open doors. Once he was back in San Diego, he found a host of people wanted to work at any job they could to get in the craft industry.

Thomas got some good advice from a family friend who was already in the craft business. Make a decision, she told him. Did he want to be in sales or a brewer? If he was clear about what he wanted, he could move forward.

In San Diego, he got an assistant brewing position at Rock Bottom. Unlike at a big facility where jobs are specialized, employees learn 100 percent of the job at a smaller brewpub. Thomas learned formulation, ordering, and line clearing. It was one-stop shop training.

A year into the job, he was promoted to running the Rock Bottom location at Long Beach in Los Angeles for a year and a half.

The opportunity to move to Nashville opened in 2014. He and his wife jumped out of the concrete jungle and moved down South to a different culture.

Thomas had to adjust his brewing to the South and the tourist area of Nashville, which was accustomed to a ton of domestic beer drinkers. He brought his recipes from the West Coast with him—a Scotch ale, a jalapeno lager, and others.

Part of Rock Bottom is a chain-style restaurant. Even though there is a legit local brewery connected to the restaurant, the clientele perceives it as a corporate business—but not the beers.

The Rock Bottom in Nashville used to be part of Big River, also a restaurant that brewed house beers. Rock Bottom bought it out in 1994. The ten-barrel brewhouse is the oldest in the city. It is so old and rickety that it's loud and vibrates, and its nickname is the Millennium Falcon. It drives the brewing team nuts looking for consistency and variable control, but no matter the problems, the beer turns out great every time.

Neil Fisher of WeldWerks Brewing Company (Greely, Colorado)

When Neil Fisher attended college in Chapel Hill, North Carolina, in 2003, craft beer intrigued him, but there wasn't a lot of it around.

North Carolina "popped the cap" in 2005, allowing beer with an ABV greater than 6 percent. With the previous limits, there were few craft breweries.

The brewing process interested Neil, as did the products, which were different from those made by big beer companies. The culture was more about enjoying the beer than consuming it.

He moved to Colorado in 2008 and experienced a totally different landscape with an active homebrew scene, and all the local breweries made amazing beer. It was an opportunity as a consumer to learn more about what he enjoyed and what made breweries attractive.

Neil jumped into homebrewing with both feet. He brewed in the kitchen for the first time, but it made such a mess that he moved into the garage. His wife was amazingly supportive when he bought a turkey fryer and spent too much money upgrading the equipment.

He doesn't like doing things by himself, and he always found a friend or two to help with his projects. Soon fifteen people were coming to the garage to help brew and drink the beer. They watched sports and connected in community, an informal homebrew club, even though there were already two homebrew clubs in town. He met his current business partner, Colin Jones, in that informal homebrew club.

Comradery was the goal and the motivation to continue brewing. He also wanted to make better beer.

Some of the guys pitched in for ingredients, but Neil covered much of the cost. For the others, it was essentially free. A bunch of guys drinking free beer together will naturally start coming up with great ideas, such as the one that Neil should start his own brewery.

Neil saw two problems. First, people think that free beer tastes better than it does. Second, opening a brewery is a business and a whole different animal.

Neil Fisher and Colin Jones of WeldWerks.
Courtesy WeldWerks Brewing.

However, he was always interested in the idea of opening a brewery, but it would take a lot more than buddies saying he made good beer. Neil and Colin made an informal betting agreement: if they won a medal at a bigger, regional homebrew competition (not something local), then they would take the idea seriously.

January 2014 arrived, and they went to the Big Beers Fest competition in Vail, Colorado. The competition was for homebrewers only. The connection and networking with others who shared the same passion inspired the guys, and, more importantly, they took two medals home that first year.

Okay, Neil thought. Maybe it was more than just a few guys at the house who liked it.

The culture of Colorado is different than that of North Carolina or Georgia. There are fewer people, but more of them drink craft beer, which has been part of the culture since Coors days and with all the breweries in the state. The legislation was advantageous and the landscape beneficial. It would be easier to start a brewery there but more difficult to grow it.

If they wanted to open a brewery, it had to be something that could grow and thrive rather than simply exist, which was tough to do when there were so many options. What would make them different and help them stand out?

They knew it had to be the product. That came first. They wanted to be known for quality. Neil and Colin won at another regional homebrew competition and medaled at the Homebrew ProAm. Cresting that wave, they moved forward with their plans.

Neil had ten different barrels in his basement for barrel-aged beers, which was unique for a homebrewer, and he found opportunities to write beer articles. Making a name as a homebrewer made him more attractive to banks and investors; it gave him more legitimacy than simply a hobbyist turning pro.

Neil and Colin started their business plan in April 2014 and opened WeldWerks in February 2015. Six months in, they won a medal at the Great American Beer Fest, and then at the World Beer Cup, continuing to maintain their commitment to quality.

Whit Baker of Bond Brothers Beer Company
(Cary, North Carolina)

Whit Baker taught high school chemistry for seven years. A friend taught him to brew at home. As a huge nerd, Whit loved brewing, and it made him want to figure out the science behind it. However, the end goal wasn't finding the answer to x, it was quality and enjoyment. Unlike genetics or math, it wasn't about getting a specific right answer but about tweaking elements to make better-tasting beer.

He is a certified beer judge and has other national certifications for beer. His drive for homebrewing was always about creating great tasting beverages he could be proud of.

While working on his brewing craft, Whit connected with Jeremy and Jason Bond. A fourth homebrewer, Andy Schnitzer, approached them and said he had a space that would be good for a brewery. Maybe they would all like to open a brewery together?

Their answer was yes.

Bond Brothers opened in February 2016.

Like the other breweries, Bond Brothers has its own story that led the owners to an alternate and independent business.

ALTERNATE AND INDEPENDENT

Everyone loves to root for the underdog.

A revolution needs a villain, something or someone to fight against, or, more importantly, something to fight for, a cause to unify the members.

For those in craft brewing, the big beer conglomerates, such as Busch, Pabst, Miller, and others, fill the role of a villain. What better enemy could exist? They are massive companies with billions of dollars in marketing and brewing factories that pump out millions of gallons of beer. They're corporations that are interested in quantity over quality. Their obsession with being the biggest and best squeezed local saloons of the late 1800s and early 1900s into considering illegal activities to stay afloat, which further fed and confirmed the demonization attempted by the Temperance movement and Know Nothing Party.

After Prohibition, these big names were the few breweries to survive, and they had the clout to pressure the legal system to give them advantages, as large companies often do. The resulting cheap and shrink-wrapped consumer mentality of the next generation through the 1950s and 1960s finished off most of the rare, small, local or even regional breweries in the US.

Worse, the laws of Prohibition changed, but the negative views stuck around, especially in the South, associating alcohol and beer with crime, abuse, and delinquency—and each state has its own holdouts from that time.

Of course, there's no greater crime to a craft brewer than making piss-poor beer.

Just as subcultures emerge to challenge dominant views, craft brewing developed as a distinctly American movement, much like the Colonialists reclaiming their freedom from the British Empire.

Only this time, the revolution began without any shots fired. Young people found their way by embracing ideals opposite from those of the big beer companies: local business, independence, quality, community, moderation, and collaboration.

Pioneers such as Fritz Maytag and Anchor Brewing created legends. Charlie Papazian and homebrewers multiplied through pamphlets and self-published papers.

They were alternative. Independent.

These ideas appeal to consumers such as me. When I travel to a new city or town, I ask a simple question: What place do the locals love? That's where I want to go. Even the manager of a chain brewery and restaurant supports that principle.

Economic Effects

Thomas Mercado of Rock Bottom has noticed the change and growth of the craft industry. In 2010, he attended a beer fest on a naval battleship in San Francisco. Only seventy-five people attended the event, and thirty breweries served their beers. An eighties hair band played covers, and every attendee was free to explore the ship, including the kitchen and turrets. Military police worked as security.

It was a great time. But Thomas saw a picture of the same fest in 2019, and the ship was packed, with people shoulder to shoulder.

He feels that the economic recession had a lot to do with the growth of the craft beer boom around 2010. With unemployment to underemployment and rising gas prices, people didn't have the money or margin to go on vacations or buy other leisure items. They could, however, look at normal experiences and find ways to treat themselves.

Companies found ways to elevate those normal experiences, such as movie theaters with reclining seats and table service. The Food Network boomed and helped develop people's interest in better-quality products. Consumers searched for these experiences, willing to spend more money at neighborhood restaurants owned by local entrepreneurs or on a six-pack of Sierra Nevada over Miller Lite.

In that context, craft beer was one of the only industries to grow during the recession. Thomas says that beer is recession proof. When people get depressed or feel stuck, they want to drink to drown their woes, which was another advantage craft beer had during that time.

Additionally, craft beer has an edge and a mantra to it—anti-norm, more flavor, less corporate feel.

Thomas is a true believer. He wants to support local businesses over big conglomerates whenever possible. He makes choices along those lines, voting with his dollar. That comes from being raised in the Bay Area and going to college in San Francisco, a hotbed for that anti-corporate culture mentality.

There is a statement behind craft beer, and craft beer is an accessible way to make that statement every day.

The Local Character

The term "local" has changed over time. At one point, it meant something that was made locally, with the ingredients coming from all over the country and maybe the world. Some take an extreme view, where even the ingredients should be grown and produced locally. The breweries that subscribe to that make a "total local" beer.

A lot of the best ingredients aren't local, however, and the products made in the backyard can also be more expensive. Ingredients such as hops and grains from other parts of the country cost less and are of higher quality. Is compromising aspects such as taste and cost worth being "total local"? Every brewery makes those kinds of decisions.

Whit Baker uses a local maltster in Durham when he can, but the focus for Bond Brothers is on brewing a variety of beers, the widest selection in the area—German pilsner, clear IPA, two hazy IPAs, barrel-aged sours, a blond barrel-aged sour, tangerine gose, a regular stout, cinnamon-roll stout, and others. They offer beers that are wildly unique along with traditional styles.

Bigger Isn't Better

When pairing food with beer, there are assumptions, much as there are with wine. That sensibility is changing; as beer becomes more complex and sophisticated through the craft movement, more types of food exist to pair with beer. Education becomes important, as well, to teach people how sophisticated beer has become.

At Liquid Bread, where the brewery is housed with a restaurant, people are encouraged to explore combinations of beer and food.

Refreshing beer from Liquid Bread.
Courtesy Liquid Bread Brewing.

Suggestions are made, but customers are asked what they might like and what sounds good to them.

Liquid Bread's passion is taste and flavor, not volume, and people don't always realize that bigger isn't better. Customers ask owners Brendan Arnold and Chuck Comeau to bottle and distribute their best beers, but that requires a commitment and investment to mass production that, if left unchecked, compromises what they feel makes them special.

As the craft beer industry grows, other brewers are churning out similar brews, many of them high quality. What makes Liquid Bread special and unique is its location and the customer experience, so Brandon and Chuck intentionally limit their beer to that one location. If you want to experience great beer, then you have to come to them.

They are tempted, for economic reasons, to grow and expand. When they see their numbers go down as more breweries enter the market, the knee-jerk reaction is to grow bigger. But Liquid Bread's purpose is great beer. That is their ultimate goal.

There will always be people who like great beer, and that's what they want to serve.

Express Yourself

Craft beer is the perfect outlet for expressing your core values.

Other people have different values and can express them in what they produce, creating a wide variety in the same medium.

Local breweries are rooted in the surrounding neighborhoods and communities. That helps make them unique. The name of Dino Radosta's brewery is White Street because it is on White Street, a major street through downtown Wake Forest, North Carolina, and that reflects his desire to help the community.

In the craft-industry fight against big beer, there was a push a couple years ago at the Brewers Association and the craft brewers conference that touched on the topic of quality.

It is great to make beer and to make it yourself, but the focus must be on quality. What if a brewery isn't concerned with quality? Just as a great experience can convert customers, a bad one can also turn

Enter the doors to the White Street Brewery.
Courtesy White Street Brewing.

them off. These customers would leave with the perception that craft beer isn't worth the time.

That can have as much of a detrimental effect to the industry as a convert's positive experience does for the good, if not more so because of existing domination by big beer companies. The way to win against bad beer isn't with more bad beer. Minds will change with great experiences and beer that no one can deny is amazing.

The craft industry can't have beer that sucks. It hurts everyone.

Iconic Names

Craft beer is about personality, which brewers infuse into what they brew and what they name their creations.

At Port City, Bill Butcher's commitment is to quality. From day one, he employed an experienced team of brewers led by a veteran brewmaster, all of whom were singularly focused on quality and consistency.

Port City production in Alexandria, Virginia.
Courtesy Port City Brewing.

Sit down and have a brew at Ass Clown.
Courtesy LunahZon Photography.

With Port City's decision to distribute, those elements became paramount. Customers know that they will get great quality beer that is true to style when the Port City name is on the label.

Port City has twelve different styles on the market at a time, each one an excellent example of the beer and authentically true to its style and history. Port City's products work as blueprints for styles to educate people about what a pale ale is or what a porter or hoppy lager is supposed to taste like.

The brand is iconic and recognizable, with names such as Optimal Wit, which evokes a sense of well-being, and Monumental IPA, associated with a feeling of importance and meaning that is tied to the monuments of Washington, DC.

For Matt Glidden at Ass Clown, the point of the name was to get attention. Some people in the Bible Belt don't like it, but that's okay. Matt isn't trying to make everyone happy. Others love it. He believes that if he keeps focusing on the beer, Ass Clown will keep brewing better and better products, and the brewery will grow from that.

The Craft Beer Effect

What is the importance of "local"? Most of the evidence is anecdotal rather than hard numbers. We can find those hard numbers on chain restaurants, but we can't find reliable data from small local businesses and breweries.

If we look at grocery chains and how they market their products, however, we see that even large conglomerates are appropriating words such as "independent," "craft," and "microbrew" in advertising their mass-produced brews. That suggests that those ideas are important to consumers, because those million-dollar marketing plans wouldn't bother with the concepts otherwise. They take their cues from small breweries that are doing something well.

Big conglomerates buying up independent breweries is further evidence of small-brewery success. The larger companies wouldn't do that unless they saw an advantage.

It doesn't always work, however. A large brand recently paid a premium price for an independent brewery but couldn't maintain growth. It lost that ineffable element that spoke of quality and the message of craft brewing. It is difficult to grow large and maintain the cool factor of a local treasure.

It's about a Revolution

Josh Deth put the message in the name of his brewery—Revolution.

He speaks of the definite counterculture in craft beer. It's an independent and alternative thing to get into—but with it gaining in popularity, is it alternative anymore? Still, the idea of being part of something different appealed to Josh.

The name of his brewery—Revolution—is a tribute to what craft beer is all about and his own background in community organizing.

Distinctive taps at Revolution.
Courtesy Revolution Brewing.

An appreciation for history balances the independent and open-mindedness of craft beer. Brewers want to both innovate and connect with the history of beer, exploring and resurrecting old styles and ways.

When starting his brewery, Josh knew how many breweries failed in the late 1990s, but he also knew there was still room for more. He researched the mistakes others made that he could avoid. He decided to do it better.

Now Revolution Brewing is the largest independent craft brewery in Illinois. For a time, it was the fastest growing. It went from being an upstart to one of the most recognized breweries as it approaches its ten-year anniversary in 2019.

Their neighborhood in Chicago is changing and gentrifying. Revolution gets both credit and blame. They spurred retail development on Milwaukee Avenue, once a classic commercial street. They are an urban brewery, and that determines much of their character and direction.

Due to the influence of Revolution, Chicago now has more breweries than any major city in the country.

Revolution makes several different styles of beer but focuses on IPAs. When you visit, you can have a nice kettle sour, and then move into well-balanced beers, which are great interpretations of classic styles. The barrel-aged beer program has won awards. Revolution expanded to two locations, and a wall with eleven hundred bourbon barrels is visible at the taproom in the big brewery.

It takes time to develop a barrel program. People expect the barrel-aged beers on opening day, but it doesn't work that way. Revolution used the barrel wood to open the brewpub, decorating the walls with staves of wood. They make some of the best barrel-aged beers available. People line up at the bar to get them.

Not Watered Down

Shaun Yasaki at Noble Beast doesn't know if the "local" mentality is a conscious decision for some people. It is ingrained in the fabric of craft brewing. People who want to be alternative and independent don't have to say they're going to do it. They just do it. They just *are*.

Look at how big beer is watered down, both literally and figuratively. At one point, individual breweries with character thrived in cities, but industrialization and commercialization rewarded the watered-down version of beer we get today from those companies that were out to give us the cheapest available product.

Shaun believes we're getting back to what beer was initially supposed to be. Looking at the older European styles is part of the fun, since so many became extinct through the sixties, seventies, and eighties. Noble Beast enjoys bringing the history and the old styles back. One of Shaun's favorite aspects of the brew business is making a style that is no longer popular and bringing it back to a community.

Not Looking to Sell

When navigating his business plan, Neil Fisher of WeldWerks focused on making beer as good or better than anyone else. Around the time he opened, other breweries seemed to focus on styles or regions. He thought about what he liked making and what he would focus on. It could be anything, but he wanted it executed at the highest level, adding some level of innovation.

Neil's commitment to quality was so important that WeldWerks built a financial cushion into the budget to dump beer that didn't meet the expectations. Those were hard decisions, dumping beer and money down the drain, but, after a year of consistency, WeldWerks established a reputation for always having great beer.

For a few years, WeldWerks got away from innovation, but it has recently returned to it. It is known for tackling unusual styles with unusual ingredients—not using them as gimmicks but having fun as artists with beer and doing it really well.

Consolidation is a hot topic, but WeldWerks is locally owned and not looking to sell.

It is connected to the community. Being small and flexible allows it to adapt to the changes in the market. Larger entities have more difficulty adapting.

A beautiful brew at WeldWerks.
Courtesy WeldWerks Brewing.

WeldWerks prioritizes the quality of life for its employees. It invests in higher pay, education, and long-term opportunities, making the brewery a great place to be and work. The longer an employee works for the brewery, the better the brewery becomes. The business couldn't do it without them, and the employees aren't expendable.

Neil has backed out of the brewing side of the business because his role is now vision and culture development, defining who the brewery is. The three legs of his vision are community, quality, and innovation.

Change Your Idea of Success

You have to change your idea of what success is, John Reynolds at Slow Pour says. People are less likely to start a brewery today and make millions of dollars from it.

He wouldn't go back to corporate America for anything. This is his dream job. It is hard work, but since he loves it, it is worth it.

Back when he worked for corporate America, he went on vacation with his family. He had the money and perks to take amazing vacations. But on the second-to-last day of the holiday, he experienced the end-of-vacation blues and dreaded going back to work. The last day would be horrible, ruined.

With Slow Pour, when he is on vacation, he can't wait to get back to work.

People are attracted to passion. The brewer asks John what he should brew. John's response is, "What do you want to brew?" While they brew some standards, the brewer has a lot of latitude in what beers to make. John believes that they should brew what they're passionate about, and the passion will brew great products. That passion comes through. People can taste it.

Like Going to Church

Jeff Erway at La Cumbre remembers the first time he went to Sierra Nevada Brewing. He thought he was in church. "This is my home," he thought.

The patio and sign for La Cumbre in Albuquerque, New Mexico.
Courtesy Cory Campbell.

Over the years, he's known people who work there, including the owners, and they are amazing people. He didn't get into the industry to make millions of dollars. The passion and the cooperation inspired him. He hopes that there's still plenty of room for everyone to express their individual artistry and make a living.

With His Own Hands

There's nothing that gives a place character like building it with your own hands.

Walt Wooden built the picnic tables that went on the patio and worked on the brews before StillFire opened its doors. A local artisan constructed the long tables, complete with USB outlets, in the tap-room. While they had to gut the inside of the old fire station, they

Have a brew at StillFire.
Courtesy Karl Lamb.

Werk Force Werktoberfest.
Courtesy Amanda Wright.

kept as much of the character as they could, connecting with the first responder community.

As Werk Force grew, Brandon Wright knew they needed to move to a bigger space.

At the end of the building, a CrossFit center had to downsize and move. The landlord offered the space to Brandon, and Werk Force transitioned from 3,500 square feet to 10,000. Brandon sat down with the bank and financed a new ten-barrel brewhouse with fermentation tanks, glycol, and everything else he needed.

With the loan spent on the equipment, he didn't have the money to build out the new space. He had to do it himself from the ground up. Fortunately, Brandon's father and grandfather were good with tools and construction. When he was a kid, Brandon had spent time with his dad in the garage building toys, model cars, and model airplanes.

Rather than hiring contractors to do the build out, he went to Home Depot, bought a nail gun and compressor and supplies and built the brewery over eight months. He hung drywall, built the bar and tables, and made light fixtures from bourbon barrels. Similar light fixtures can cost $500 each, but he watched YouTube videos and made them himself. He had to hire guys for the concrete, electrical, and plumbing, but he did much of the work.

Much of it, but not all. His friends and father came to help. His wife hung scaffolding and painted with safe paint when she was eight months pregnant.

Now they have a spacious brewery with history and a story within each decoration and fixture, along with each beer and brew, creating a place for people to meet and connect.

THE GATHERING

Craft beer isn't about drinking alone.

A comedian, Sebastian Maniscalco, has an interesting bit about what it was like when someone rang the doorbell twenty years ago versus today. Two decades ago, our mothers had different dishes for company. They had a dessert or a dish of some sort ready just in case company came over. And when the doorbell rang, we all got excited. Who was it? Who had come over? When we answered the door, the person or family visiting would say they were in the neighborhood. We invited them in and had conversation over coffee or tea and the special dish our mothers had put aside.

Now? If someone pulls up to the driveway, we get nervous. Who is it? Who knows we're here? Maybe we turn out the lights or hide, and maybe we don't even answer the door.

A few years ago, I wrote an article that contrasted the front porch and the back deck. We had a front porch when I was a kid. My dad put a bench swing out there, and we actually sat on it, swinging and talking as a family. I played with Transformers and G.I. Joes and Hot Wheels on the porch. Neighbors walked by, and we'd wave or invite them over to play there with us. The front porch communicated a welcoming feeling.

Decades passed, and cultures changed. New houses rarely have front porches, but more of them have back decks. We grill burgers and hot dogs, maybe hang out on comfy chairs around a fire pit where no one can see us and where we don't have to wave at or see anyone else, and our neighbors aren't invited over.

We have become a more isolated culture. People still desire those times of community, however. Connection is ingrained in our DNA. So where do we find those connections now?

This can explain the rise of town squares in suburban areas, the attraction of a third-wave coffee shop, and the reach of Meetup groups . . . and craft breweries.

The initial motivation from Fritz Maytag, Charlie Papazian, and the other founders of the craft beer industry was to make beer that they liked to drink. The idea of community correlated to that in a very real way. A homebrewer today can check out YouTube videos and find articles and recipes online and never have to meet a soul. In the 1970s, homebrewing was illegal, and it spread by word of mouth and by gathering in basements, garages, or backyards to show off concoctions and share the newest trick someone found. Pamphlets were printed and handed out or mailed.

As those in the craft industry dug back into history to rediscover old styles of beer or visited Europe to experience better beer and the culture there, the old notion of a neighborhood pub or social house to get together over a brew was also restored to the national conscience.

A further example of rebellion against the norm and American big beer consumerism, craft beer is about the experience, gathering with friends, using beer as a tool to begin a conversation. Breweries become spaces where the community congregates for life events and where kids and dogs are often welcome—where we can be friends and neighbors again.

The Beer Solution to the Divide

John Reynolds worked in tech for fifteen years. It paid the bills, but he knew the downside of technology. It is very divisive.

There's no reason to leave the house anymore, with our big screen TVs and surround sound; we enjoy ultimate comfort in every room. We can have our meals and groceries delivered. Any product can be shipped—for free, most of the time—right to our front door and cheaper than going to the store. Plus, we save time.

The taproom at Slow Pour.
Courtesy Slow Pour Brewing.

But we've lost the value of experiencing our community. We don't get to have meaningful conversations. People don't even know how to have them anymore.

In contrast, John's brewery, Slow Pour, doesn't have any TVs. They have one screen that drops down, only for a big event such as a championship game that everyone watches together.

You can't hold your phone with a beer in your hand. People can walk into Slow Pour, have a beer with people they've never met before, and leave with some sense of community. There is value in sitting down with someone you wouldn't otherwise encounter and having a beer and a conversation.

The technology of cell phones and social media only compounds the problem. We pick teams before we even meet anyone else—political, religious, or sports teams, it doesn't matter. We make assumptions about others before having a real conversation with them. We don't take the time to know them as individuals. Because of tech and isolation, we begin relationships already at odds.

Breweries offer an alternative to that. Put down our phones. Sit where there aren't any screens at a long table across from others and hear their stories. We can tell our stories. We begin as friends.

John went to Guatemala a few years ago, and the overwhelming sense of community struck him. There were several differences from America. There were economic factors, of course, but the American higher standard of living comes with a price—more technology and increased isolation.

Walking through an area of Guatemala, he saw a little girl taking care of other little kids from the community, as though she was responsible for their well-being. He was jealous of that sense of community, where everyone is your family.

John believes that the best way to experience a place or culture is through its food. A brewery must maintain that local character and flavor to help visitors know what is important and unique about that town or community.

The Slow Pour space has a history to it. It's an older, restored building in an old part of the city of Lawrenceville, Georgia. It reaches back to a time when the business wasn't about bars and getting drunk but about beer halls and social houses.

It is kid and dog friendly, with dog treats, craft sodas, and board games. The Slow Pour slogan is "the moment matters."

John is also a man of faith, and in suburban Atlanta, Georgia, he is often asked about how he can balance his religious beliefs with making beer. Of course people can misuse and abuse anything, he concedes, but that's not the intent.

Prohibition used an extreme solution that didn't solve the problem. Crime increased, far more than anyone expected. Making alcohol illegal obviously wasn't the solution. But there were serious issues with saloons and guzzling bars. The solution was to change the thinking and culture around alcohol, not demonize it.

It is cost prohibitive to go to a craft brewery to get drunk. The price of a beer alone discourages it, not to mention the environment, where everyone is welcome and kids and dogs are present.

The beer and ingredients are designed for people to experience something of quality. To John, if someone walks in and drinks a beer and that's all they do, shame on them. The brewery is about more than sitting on a couch and drinking alone. Between the interactions with the staff, sitting in the space with lights bouncing off the walls, and a local musician playing, Slow Pour isn't selling beer but an experience, inclusion in a community. Beer just helps that happen.

John doesn't want to simply exist in a space. He wants to have active participation and be a part of the community. The brewery is passionate about finding ways to give back to the community by trying to partner with a nonprofit every month.

There is bingo night every month, and 100 percent of the proceeds go to a nonprofit, such as the Village of Hope or the Lawrenceville Co-Op. The prizes at bingo are donated by partners in the city. Those nights help bring awareness and resources to those nonprofits.

Simple Southernality is a music fest Slow Pour holds every spring, where popular local groups play. It rained on the day of the event in 2019 when they were expecting six thousand people. They rented a forty-by-eighty-foot tent, and over three thousand people attended. It is a free show that partners with the city of Lawrenceville. Slow Pour doesn't make money, but that's not the point. It is a way to celebrate the community and showcase local talent in food, music, and beer.

Slow Pour has its regulars, great people who have supported them since they opened a few years ago. The design for the taproom was intentional, with tables, chairs, and couches. John wanted it to have a living room atmosphere, so customers would feel like they're at home. The brewery belongs to the customers. Slow Pour is just there to help facilitate that community.

Designing with Intention

No TVs in the taproom was an early decision for Brandon Wright at WerkForce. First, he and his wife hated when they went out to eat and people sat there staring at TVs around them or at their phones, not talking to each other. Communication is a lost art in our culture, he believes.

The community at the taproom at Werk Force.
Courtesy Amanda Wright.

Second, Brandon is a bluegrass, roots Americana, Deadhead kind of guy. He's not into popular sports; he'd rather go fishing, skateboarding, or snowboarding. When people come into the brewery, they will invariably hear roots Americana music or a Grateful Dead show from 1978.

WerkForce is a community center, like an old German beer hall. All the tables are long to encourage people to sit together. They look at the beer through the lens of the past. Families gather together in the common room.

Through Prohibition, that community element was lost, and people ended up looking at bars as places to get drunk and get rid of their problems. Plainfield, Illinois, has embraced the idea of community. It is an old mining village, so serving beer without serving food was considered a big concern to the locals. Brandon was fingerprinted for the liquor license, and the officer looked at him and commented on how they didn't normally give places without food a liquor license.

It took time, but now the town understands that the brewery doesn't attract the drunks. The craft beer culture is different. They close at 10:00 p.m. and don't deal with the late crowd. WerkForce doesn't want to introduce that into the community. Since they allow kids and dogs, Fridays and Saturdays are filled with families and people talking with one another—people from newborns to those ninety years old and from all walks of life. The community now thanks WerkForce for their influence.

Brandon and WerkForce also give back by having a community pool of cash. They started by paying bartenders higher wages than required. In addition, a portion of the tips goes to charities, such as for children battling cancer or helping a woman whose apartment burned down. She lost everything, and they put the first month's rent down for her.

Every month, they rotate to give to a different charity, and, each year, WerkForce donates thirty Thanksgiving turkeys to the local turkey drive. A different jar sits separate from the one for tips, and local people are asked to put in money for charity. The brewery has produced a special beer and given proceeds from it to the local community.

WerkForce tends to give to individuals rather than to bigger organizations.

Once or twice a month, a bluegrass band plays a free concert for the taproom for fun. The brewery has hosted a disc golf swap where vendors bought, sold, and swapped the discs. WerkForce also brings in food trucks over the weekend.

The Best-Kept Secret

Ass Clown is off the beaten path and hard to find. They were able to have food trucks in the beginning, but the local owners' association didn't like that. They also weren't allowed to have an outdoor area. Matt Glidden considers it lucky that Ass Clown still around, especially now that most breweries are moving toward being more like public houses.

Craft beer isn't about quantity. People come into the brewery and drink one or two beers and leave to eat somewhere else. Perhaps they

Playing Jenga at Ass Clown.
Courtesy LunahZon Photography.

order in from DoorDash or Uber Eats, which helps the brewery by keeping people on site. Matt hopes to add more food and community options during the week.

When they were decorating Ass Clown, they used whatever was free—pallets, coffee bags, and more. They used to have small tables, but now that the bar is bigger, they've added eclectic stools and furniture. Like the name, the brewery infused the decorations and layout of the taproom with their personality.

Matt is big on giving back to the community and gives to different nonprofits. Ass Clown does all it can, and that aspect grows as they do.

The regulars come in and talk to the bartenders about the brews and what they like. The bartenders leave notes at the end of their shifts based on the regulars' feedback. This helps the brewer dial in the recipe. With a name like Ass Clown, they sell a lot of merchandise, as well.

Freedom Creates Community

Noble Beast Brewing Company only has one regularly scheduled event, trivia on Tuesdays, and the same crowd, teams of friends, comes in each week to compete. Other than that event, the community at the brewery is organic. Shaun Yasaki doesn't look for ways to draw a crowd.

While they have a kitchen, Noble Beast doesn't operate like a restaurant, which sometimes leads to negative reviews. People order both food and drinks at the bar, and then the orders are brought out to them. At busy times, it is difficult to order and get food quickly.

At a typical restaurant, a host seats the customers, and the expectation is that they will sit, eat, drink, and then leave. The restaurant model is about turning tables for more money.

Community fosters a different environment, one where people can connect. At Noble Beast, customers have the freedom to move tables and chairs around, and that contributes to a slowed-down, laid-back vibe within the taproom. The taproom constantly shifts, as friends hang out and more come in, the tables and groups growing or moving as needed throughout the night.

The brewery is in downtown Cleveland, Ohio, on the edge of the business district, surrounded by companies rather than residential homes or apartments. Many of the regulars come in for lunch.

Shaun leans heavily on what he wants to brew. He has a reputation for tackling styles that aren't the most popular. He convinces people to drink those strange beers through the power of story behind them. Stories are how people connect, and beer styles have history. The innovations by people such as Shaun have stories, too, which adds to the experience of having a local craft beer.

The Tourist Struggle

Rock Bottom has won hundreds of awards at the Great American Beer Fest—not easy medals to win—and the brewery is a great training ground for brewers. The craft culture at Rock Bottom in Tennessee is a struggle, however, as customers perceive the local brewery as being corporate and nothing more.

Rock Bottom's unique marriage of chain restaurant and local brewery makes it the first step in craft beer for many. The establishment offers an unpretentious, comfortable situation for the non-craft beer consumer. Rock Bottom easily attracts the craft consumer too, because the beer is high quality.

Thomas Mercado and Rock Bottom might miss out on some aspects of craft culture, such as lines around the block when they introduce a new beer. But the purpose of Rock Bottom is to offer non-craft consumers the opportunity to come into a craft establishment (that also sells wine and liquor) and slowly chip away at their presumptions about beer.

Their number-one selling beer is the Southern Flier, a craft American light lager, which is a crisp and smooth beverage people consistently love. Rock Bottom is in a great position as the tip of the spear, often the first to get people to try craft beers. Beer consumption massively favors domestic big beer and imports. Those domestic drinkers are comfortable in chain restaurants. For the older generation and blue-collar workers, Rock Bottom offers the comfortable, chain-restaurant feel that can introduce them to something independent.

The staff is trained to keep their noses pointed down. They learn not to be condescending or pretentious about what the beer is. Consumers won't be converted to craft beer if the staff is rude and obnoxious about it. The staff must be welcoming and understanding to people who are unaccustomed to the more diverse flavor profiles of craft beer.

Take Time and Slow Down

Whit Baker connects the laid-back mentality of craft beer with the larger slow food movement in general. People desire quality and experience without the rush or mass marketing. Slow food, with its expensive ingredients, comes at a higher cost, however. Craft beer allows the same quality irrespective of volume; the brewer can make more of it at a lower cost.

The taproom at Bond Brothers is a place to slow down, gather, and enjoy a high-quality product. The taps keep the beer fresh at a reasonable price and hits a sweet spot of local or hyperlocal.

When you go out to a restaurant, you know who you're going to sit with and talk to. That's part of the choice. At a taproom, there is no assigned seating. It is casual, and formality is dropped in new conversations and friends.

Bond Brothers does a great deal of fund-raising and holds several events out of the brewery. Much of the local support comes from 5Ks and a one-thousand person running club. All four owners are runners, so it's natural for them to have that connection to the community. They started the club once the brewery opened.

Community events are held in a side room. The number of meetings has increased so much that they had to hire an events coordinator. Unlike other eateries or even bars or wineries, a brewery and taproom is locked into the community. The town sees it as a neighborhood space and wants to have its events there. The inclusion of dogs and kids in the taproom gives a welcoming feel to the space, as well. It becomes an intersection of all the things that people like. The brewery doesn't have a barrier to entry.

It doesn't have an adult or bar feel to it. There's no hard liquor. No one is getting hammered. It's a place for groups and friends to interact in a positive environment.

Part of the Community

StillFire also has events on a regular basis. The main taproom is set aside for major events, such as corporate parties or library events for a new book about Georgia brewing. With their premium location near both the downtown park and surrounding houses and condos, StillFire sees a cross section of the community every night and over the weekend.

On Friday and Saturday nights, local musicians and bands play for the crowd, and on other nights, the customers can enjoy trivia or poker nights. The taproom is dog friendly, and one evening, a local animal

Sunshine in the taproom at StillFire.
Courtesy Karl Lamb.

organization brought in puppies that people could cuddle for a dona-
tion. Dog treats and water bowls are placed around the taproom.

Food is catered in on busy nights, supporting local restaurants, but
many customers order pizzas or bring their own food, as well. Regulars have birthday parties or other life events at the long tables. On
nights when the taproom is rented out, StillFire has a to-go window
that serves the patio and park.

The Founders Club at StillFire began when the brewery opened last
year as a way to help invest in the brewery. With this VIP membership,
"founders" get their own beer glasses on the wall and one free beer
each day or night they come in. Other perks are included, and it's been
popular. One founder has been there every day that they've been open!

StillFire holds amazing parties for the community, such as Super
Bowl or Valentine's Day, in a packed taproom. The brewers, including
Phil Ferril and Walt Wooden, take breaks from the brewhouse to walk
around, talk to people, and get feedback on the brews.

Because it was a former fire station, the brewery is located between city hall and the police station, further connecting them to the community.

A Bigger Table

To foster more community, most taprooms have gone to bigger tables that force people to sit together instead of at separate, smaller tables. Port City wants their customers to have an interactive experience. They have a great crowd of regular customers who come in after work with friends or who sit with new friends they've made in the taproom. On weekends, more patrons come from out of town.

Port City is open seven days a week. On Monday, people can join the fun run with Joggers and Lagers, sponsored by a local running store. The run begins at 7:00 a.m. and stretches for a three- or five-mile loop that starts and ends at the brewery. Runners can come in and have a pint when they're done. Beer Yoga has been going for over seven years. Thirty to forty people line up on Tuesdays and pay for forty-five minutes of yoga and a pint afterward.

Other events include monthly trivia, stand-up comedy, and a cycling event on Saturdays that starts and ends at the brewery.

The brewery gives to charities on a regular basis. They carefully choose charities with a personal connection to an employee or customer. Port City has contributed through donations, food drives, and more.

In the Local Fabric

A brewery's community isn't an out-of-the-ordinary experience. For many, it's part of a daily or weekly ritual.

Life happens at the brewery. The Courtyard has seen engagements, weddings, and even times when people mourn together. People come for business meetings or dates or after work to cool down and relax. Fund raisers occur often for local charities, such as for cancer victims, autism, or others.

The goal of customers isn't to get sloshed. The mentality is to be an adult and have a drink with friends, and then go home, healthy and normal.

When Courtyard opened, 75 to 80 percent of the customers were local and regulars, rather than visitors or people from out of town. Now it's evolved to an even split between locals and tourists and even large groups, such as bachelor parties or a bus of tourists. Fortunately, that change wasn't due to losing the locals but to becoming a destination spot for visitors to the city.

Some of Scott Wood's closest friends are brewers who often began as collaborations, meeting at a festival, hanging out, and then making beer together. He has found that craft beer tends to attract high-quality humans. They pay attention to passion and quality, and those connections create a large family where people are given the benefit of the doubt. Scott has friends across the country, but it is also a small, interconnected community. The money made in craft beer is the by-product of enjoyment and community.

Community Outreach Is Part of the Job

Neil Fisher at WeldWerks worked full time in nonprofit before opening his own brewery, and he brought those connections with Habitat for Humanity and other organizations with him into his new venture.

Their first employee is now director of operations and the biggest driver for community engagement and philanthropic efforts. The team at the brewery is dedicated to community outreach. Once a quarter, every team (taproom, sales, logistics, etc.) is responsible for finding a nonprofit to partner and volunteer with. It could be a local food bank or the aforementioned Habitat for Humanity. Production shuts down for a day, and every employee is paid to go work at that nonprofit.

This community outreach is part of the job and helps them understand what the community needs. For two years, 100 percent of the profit of one of their beers went to build a house for Habitat for Humanity.

WeldWerks created a nonprofit, WeldWerks Community Foundation, to help start the WeldWerks Invitational Festival. Inspired by

Enjoying flights together at the bar at WeldWerks.
Courtesy WeldWerks Brewing.

the Firestone Walker Brewing Company, who run their own famous beer fest in California, Neil and his partners considered putting on the festival. They put out feelers to other breweries in the state, and the overwhelming response was a resounding yes. The WeldWerks Invitational has grown. Neil and the brewery didn't want to make any profit for themselves from the $100 a ticket. They wanted to give all of it back to the community and engage people in the craft industry. All proceeds of the festival go to local nonprofits that are chosen through a grant application process.

It is crazy and cool, Neil says. They get to play Santa Claus.

The taproom at WeldWerks is kid friendly, and dogs can hang out on the patio. Regulars come to the taproom. Much of the sales comes from beer tours for out-of-town visitors or a new release.

Thursday night at the taproom has turned into a standing date for friends to meet for drinks. The brewery created a communal space that is well used by local friends. That is the heart of what craft beer is, to enjoy the beer and talk about it or about something else. Neil wants people to feel at home, like they're in their living room, so they'll connect and feel comfortable. The communal vibe is one of Neil's favorite parts of craft breweries.

Experience the Culture Firsthand

When Chuck Comeau was younger, he learned to cook by following his mother's recipes. They included innocuous statements such as, "knead until shiny." What did that mean? If she had been there to explain it, then he would have understood.

As the brewer, that's what Brendan Arnold does with clients when he shares the process of their beers, helping people to taste and sense the flavors. Much as when people go to the vineyard and learn about the aspects of the wine they should be experiencing, the customer remembers and searches for that quality in the future, and that is the real glue of creating a market.

Most of the events at Liquid Bread feature tasting the beer as opposed to simply talking about it or putting a picture of it out on social media. The proof of good beer is in the taste and the experience in the environment where it was made. Firsthand experience is the ultimate goal.

When Chuck and Brendan first started Liquid Bread, they tried all kinds of advertising, but the best was word of mouth. Keeping customers happy and helping them enjoy the whole experience was better than worrying about how many likes and connections they had on Facebook or email. The brewery has stuck to focusing on a great experience, and they promote the events in-house and through word of mouth.

Liquid Bread releases a beer twice a month—New Beers Eve events—and promotes those releases with live music and free merchandise. They work closely with a chef and catering manager for special food.

Pouring a brew for a customer at Liquid Bread.
Courtesy Liquid Bread Brewing.

Brendan and Chuck feel an obligation to sit and have a beer with customers after work. That's how they get their best feedback.

New instructors from a local college came in recently, and Brendan gave them a tour and tasting. That is the real deal—interacting with local people and sharing the message and story of the brewery. Those are the clients that the brewery keeps. Liquid Bread feels that if they relied on Untappd (an app where people rate craft beers) for feedback, they'd be screwed. A personal relationship is central and valuable to their business.

A City of Neighborhoods

In a city such as Chicago, which is made up of different districts, a brewery can be a neighborhood-based business where people can meet others who live and work close to them.

Revolution hosts fund raisers and events such as weddings, but it is also a casual place to come in and have a beer or two—kind of like a corner bar. Chicago used to have a culture of corner bars, but that is fading. Generations change, and no one opens an old-time corner bar anymore. The local brewery has taken up that neighborhood function.

Chicago has a history of change, growth, and redevelopment from the fire in 1871 right through the modern day. People take risks and open businesses. If you can bring something of quality that people want, it is welcomed by the city.

Josh Deth appreciates locally made things. Before owning Revolution, he ran a farmers' market and has been involved with the chamber of commerce. People want to give their time and dollars to something local that is well made.

He didn't think there were enough local breweries. At a local beer store, the only beer he found that was made in the huge city of Chicago was Goose Island. He had traveled around the country, and there were eight craft breweries in Denver in the 1990s. Chicago was bigger than Denver but only had one or two.

With the industrial base and history, Chicago had great buildings, and Josh was motivated to create more than a brewery but a space,

Long tables at Revolution Brewing encourage customers to sit and engage with neighbors. *Courtesy Revolution Brewing.*

a place where the neighborhood could gather and experience life together. And great beer, of course.

The bartenders speak with the customers about the beer as much as the brewers do, and some of the best ideas for new beers or changes come from the bar.

Revolution has worked with charities. The community loves when they make a beer for a charity and $1 from every pint goes to those in need. That also brings in different crowds that are connected with the charity.

A perfect pint of beer is a beautiful thing on its own, but beer can be the means to other ends too. It is part of social lubrication, bringing people together.

Big time beer, small town soul at White Street.
Courtesy White Street Brewing.

A Business That Makes a Local Investment

White Street was one of the businesses to make a significant investment in downtown Wake Forest, a watershed moment that spurred economic growth. Other quality businesses, seeing the brewery as an example of success, opened downtown as well. People came downtown for a good local business such as White Street, and that sparked revitalization. Dino Radosta serves on the downtown revitalization committee, and he is involved in the chamber.

Dino and the brewery wanted to create a space where people could meet for their usual activities. Monday night is the homebrew club they sponsor, Tuesday is for the runners club, Wednesday is trivia night, and Thursday is for the bicycle club. They host programs and groups, giving people a place to meet so that people can experience what they enjoy.

It is a return to the social house idea, where they consistently make quality beer and serve in an amazing environment that the customer can count on 100 percent. White Street ensures people have nothing less than the best experiences.

The brewery is on the main drag, and they collaborated with the town to start Friday Night on White, which is a street festival. The street is shut down for two or three blocks. The brewery partners with the town to provide a band and stage with beer trucks and no other activities. It draws twelve thousand people a night.

It is amazing what a brewery can do. It's a place where people can be themselves and be with their friends. The street festival is the taproom on a mega scale.

It makes sense. Craft beer has been about collaboration from the beginning.

A CULTURE OF COLLABORATION

Capitalism has its detractors and supporters. On one hand, the freedom to innovate and compete has helped the United States raise its standard of living and influence the world. On the other hand, companies sometimes abuse the system, and innocent people feel the negative effects. Those on one extreme call for an ultimate free market for the sake of progress, while others argue for the government takeover of every industry to protect against corruption.

First- and second-generation German immigrants initiated and ran the big breweries in the mid-nineteenth century. These people had an entrepreneurial spirit and a historic perfect storm of product (a light lager) and new technology (railroads, refrigeration, etc.). At some point, the idea of capitalism was married with cutthroat competition (the Industrial Revolution and the rise of monopolies) and the desire to not only be personally successful or wealthy but to crush others in the market.

The bigger beer companies grew wealthier, and the local saloon owners were the collateral damage, pushed into choosing between closing doors or engaging in illegal activities. Those dingy places of ill repute became fodder for the propaganda of the Temperance movement and served as evidence for the ultimate passing of Prohibition.

Making alcohol illegal didn't solve the nation's moral ills. In fact, Prohibition made things worse, creating an underground black market that fed new gangs and criminal organizations with cash and power.

Craft beer is a "people's movement" that doesn't view the extremes as solutions. Its solution is a change of culture around alcohol and beer, changing the story with different perspectives instead of heavy-handed political action.

I lived in the Republic of Korea for four years. As an American, I was confused when I saw the same types of businesses every block or two—a small market, a shoe store, an underwear store, and others, repeated over and over. As I learned more about the culture, I realized that the corner market on this block and the one on the next street over didn't see each other as competitors. They were friends and part of a community. They could all succeed together.

For the craft beer culture, this was the solution for the ills of capitalism. Instead of an absolute free market with no regulation (leading to abuse) or government takeovers of industries to protect against corruption (it doesn't—it only changes the source of corruption), craft beer began a revolution based on the ideas that they could change the culture and that there was room for everyone. They changed the standard for success; instead of cutthroat competition, the craft industry is marked with collaboration and those seeking to help and share knowledge and skills with others to make great beer.

We saw it in the chapter on the community—it is a pattern that breweries are involved in charitable works and organizations, seeking to give back as much as they can. That's part of the new measure of success.

That revolution of open-handedness is connected with the desire to fight the villain of big beer, to be sure. The success of one brewery leads to success for all breweries. A person converting to craft beer gives the whole industry another customer.

But it's more than that. It's a mind-set of people who wonder if they can do business differently and aren't waiting for a government to do it for them. They actually do it. These business owners make money, pay their bills, and do more than just survive while also giving generously and sharing secrets of the trade with anyone who wants to know.

Just as the goal of the local taproom is to be a place where we see our neighbors as friends instead of enemies, the new standard of success in craft beer is viewing others as friends, partners, and neighbors instead of competitors. Breweries regularly create beers together, even calling them "collab beers."

That's my kind of revolution.

Paying It Forward

White Street only makes collab beers occasionally, but they have been recipients of the sharing within the industry. They brewed nine thousand barrels last year. Through an order mix-up, they were short a couple hundred pounds of grain. They contacted another brewery, and that "competitor" lent them what they needed. Dino Radosta says they'd do the same.

Some of that collaborative culture is completely altruistic; some is due to the common mission of growing craft beer as a whole. The industry needs more people drinking and converting, and if Dino can help another craft brewer, it ultimately benefits him too.

A homebrew club provides internship and education, improving the skills of possible future brewers. White Street has benefited from this culture and paid it forward, such as lending others hops.

The desire to grow and open production facilities can distract from that culture of collaboration, but maintaining the grassroots taproom focus of experience and community is important.

Give It Away

Before he cofounded StillFire Brewery, when Phil Ferril won homebrewers contests, someone else made his beer. At other times, he brewed a new recipe with his brewer friends on their systems. That is an interesting process because Phil had to use whatever system his friend had designed—just like if you went to someone's house to make a pizza, you'd have to use their pans and oven. Phil followed his friends' lead when he was able to brew on their pro systems, especially since they'd done all the legwork.

As Phil saw all the setups at different breweries, he couldn't help but think about what he would and wouldn't do if he had his own. All homebrew systems are based on gravity and use no pumps. Only a rare few professional breweries are set up around gravity. Phil's partner, Walt Wooden, remembers a place in Charleston that used to have a gravity-based system. People can still see the remnants of it.

Sharing a great brew at StillFire.
Courtesy Karl Lamb.

Other breweries with similar equipment to StillFire's opened their doors and showed Phil and the other brewers how to do it. They learned a great deal.

One day, StillFire needed seven bags of grain. After one call to the brewery in the next town, Slow Pour brought over the grain. It worked both ways, too. Slow Pour called and needed five gallons of glycol, and, since StillFire had a fifty-five-gallon drum, they shared it.

Popular or not, big names or not, people are willing to help.

One of the Homebrew Cons in San Diego included a preliminary event at Lost Abbey, a brewery there. There was a serious hops shortage at the time, and hops were worth more than gold. Tomme Arthur of Lost Abbey gave out eleven pounds of hops as a door prize. For a homebrewer, that would last more than a year.

Lost Abbey, like much of the industry, had been in a bind with hops, and had asked around for help. People gave them their extra hops. When Lost Abbey had some left over, they decided to pay it forward to homebrewers.

All they asked was that the homebrewers didn't sell the hops. If the homebrewers broke up those eleven pounds, they could only give the hops away and share the wealth.

The hops shortage had an interesting byproduct. Brewers started getting better and more efficient with hops when brewing IPAs.

StillFire opened in 2019, so they haven't done any collab beers yet, but they have a few lined up. It's only a matter of time before they get those made. Collab beers are a great way to do something different and fun.

Brewery Crawl

Josh Deth's email inbox is populated with questions and comments from people on the brewers' guild list. He's been on the board of Illinois Craft Brewers Guild and once hosted its office at Revolution. It was nice to give them a home until they grew enough to afford their own space.

The wall of barrels at Revolution. *Courtesy Revolution Brewing.*

Josh is familiar with the common experience of sharing ingredients, such as a particular malt or hop that a friend will share when Josh needs it. Revolution collaborates on several beers with other breweries. People move around and work at different breweries, taking what they've learned and picking up new things from others. It is an intermingling of experience that benefits all.

Some places do a brewery crawl, like a pub crawl, where people visit one brewery after another, sampling the craft brews in a town or city. Those types of events show the collaborative nature and willingness to share success through the community.

A Collab Every Week

Before WeldWerks opened, a few breweries were transparent about answering questions regarding equipment and how to scale up recipes. Beyond that, Neil Fisher didn't shadow other breweries or visit them.

Since they have opened, WeldWerks has embraced more of the collaborative culture, partnering on several beers with others. They collab on a beer almost every week—fifty a year on average. Trillium in Boston is a brewery they've recently partnered with.

Ninety-Nine Percent Jerk-Free

Scott Wood of Courtyard has noticed arrogance and entitlement creeping into the industry, but, mostly, he still sees the sharing and collaboration. He likes going to festivals to experience the comradery among breweries and brewers, especially from those out of state.

The second-coolest experience of Scott's life was when he got to put a keg on at Toronado. That was where his conversion happened years earlier, and it was special to later taste one of his beers on those taps.

It reminded him of the unique experience of making a friend and bringing people into the craft beer community. The craft fold is so big and extensive that people can sometimes take it for granted. While there are some jerks in the industry, it's still 99 percent jerk-free.

Making friends at the WeldWerks Invitational.
Courtesy WeldWerks Brewing.

Brewers help each other, and Scott has experienced this an unbe-lievable number of times. Courtyard, a small, three-barrel brewhouse, has done collaborations with Modern Times in San Diego and other big breweries that have no reason to work with them, but it is the heart of the community to make friends and work together.

These other brewers are his friends, and Scott can text them in the middle of the night, ask a random question, and they'll respond. "It's rad," he says.

There is an indescribable comfort that comes from knowing that these other brewers and successful people in the industry don't have to spend their time doing these things but choose to because the rela-tionship matters to them. The success of the whole industry matters to them. Scott's customers matter to those other brewers.

The members of craft beer care about the industry, the connections, and their beer getting to people who will appreciate it. People in the industry recognize who is of the same ilk. Even in supposedly "saturated" areas, people take care of each other like crazy.

The competition in craft beer is about making better beer than others, not in taking money or business from them. Scott loves the beer others make, but he doesn't want to make their beer. You can't be in competition when you're not trying to copy anyone else, when you're only trying to make your own beer better.

In the 1960s, the competition between the Rolling Stones and the Beatles was not about writing songs that were like each other's but about improving their own unique sound and craft. That made amazing music for everyone.

Scott only wants to make his own beer better. When every local brewer does that, it means great beer for everyone.

The Idiots

Brandon Wright with Werk Force grew up in the industry with a group of friends, all starting breweries at the same time. They call themselves the Idiots. Why? Because they say you'd have to be an idiot to be in the craft industry—they had to work so hard for so long for so little money. Once or twice a month, they drive out from Plainfield, Illinois, to Iowa and brew beers together at a farm town brewery.

Some of the beers have Star Wars themes, such as the Imperial Force, the Imperial Blockade, and the Imperial Force Strikes Back. Soon they will do a Blue Milk beer for the taproom.

Next door to Werk Force is a coffee roaster, and they are also collaborative. They've done a cupping—a tasting of coffees from different sources and roasts—in the taproom.

Quality Will Win the Day

Bill Butcher views the collaboration and support of the craft industry as being like his experience in the wine industry, where they also share

Sharing a brew in the brewhouse at Werk Force.
Courtesy Amanda Wright.

information, knowledge, and expertise. Before he opened Port City, he contacted as many breweries as possible within driving distance and asked if they would open their doors to let him look at their setup.

He found it to be a welcoming community. Bill got in the car in the morning and drove two hours to a brewery that welcomed him in and showed him the equipment. The brewer would speak about the challenges and helped Port City along the way.

Port City tries to pay that forward as much as they can. Other breweries contact them every week with questions, and Port City does their best to be supportive.

Are they worried about competition? Not really. Ultimately, quality will win the day. It was about quality from the beginning, and as long as the industry stays true to that and continues to produce excellent, quality beer in a consistent manner, customers will keep coming back.

There's always room for more. The competition isn't about making money but about who's making the best beer.

Also, Bill believes that the local Washington, DC, area can be known for that great quality, and when that happens, it will be good for everyone in the market. Port City helping other breweries is a way to help make that dream a reality.

One of the ways Port City has contributed to that collaborative culture is with a patented device they invented for dry hopping. The device (called the Hopzooka) helps to dry hop more efficiently and consistently, which leads to better quality and safety.

Dry hopping isn't innovative, but their method is. Most brewers lean a ladder against the tank, climb to the top with a bucket of hops, open the hatch, and dump the hops in. The problem is that when the hatch opens, the tank is exposed to oxygen, which degrades the quality of the beer. The beer stales quicker.

The question was how to add hops without exposing the tank to oxygen. Brewer Jonathan Reeves invented a pressure tank that blows hops in with pressure from CO_2. Port City applied for a patent almost three years ago. They made a commitment to help other breweries that wanted to use it; they made the license available without a fee.

They believe that better-quality beer is good for everyone and good for the market.

They did make a deal with a German company that builds tanks that include the Hopzooka, which earns them some money, but the ultimate goal is to be collaborative and share the technology, whereas others would have used the patent to make money from those in the industry.

The Growth of the Industry Threatens the Culture

Jeff has seen a change in the industry regarding collaboration, and, from his perspective, it coincided with a slowdown in the growth of the industry. The pie isn't growing, so people are fighting more for their piece of it.

Craft beer enjoyed unbroken growth in the early 2000s, each year growing by over 10 percent. By 2018, that shrunk to 4 percent growth, most coming from new breweries that are less than two years old. Breweries are scrambling to survive in an industry that has seen less success in the last couple of years. That has affected willingness to help and collaborate, especially in areas with higher saturation.

On an Island

Sweetwater, the original craft beer people in Georgia, assisted John and Slow Pour right off the bat. Their twenty years of experience helped when John went down to meet with them a few times. Those

Hang with the inspiration of great beer on the wall at Ass Clown. *Courtesy LunahZon Photography.*

at Sweetwater were generous and kind people. Slow Pour uses the same yeast strain as Sweetwater does, and the larger brewery shares yeast when John and his brewers need it.

Another brewery opened in a nearby city not long after Slow Pour did, and, for a couple of years, those were the only two in Gwinnett County. While there are other breweries in downtown Atlanta and the state of Georgia, Slow Pour, being in the suburbs, might as well be in another state due to the different culture and the distance of traffic. Those two breweries in Gwinnett County were on a proverbial island.

Now the county is coming into its own, with more breweries opening in different cities. With the growing economy over the last few years and the investment of that money into more common spaces such as town squares, breweries have enjoyed success and less legal resistance than they would have twenty years ago.

Open Arms

Matt Glidden of Ass Clown Brewing has often enjoyed and given help in the craft industry, such as a bag of grain or yeast or hops. Most brewers are still collaborative and willing to help other brewers out if they need something. The competition is still with the big brewers. Matt doesn't see it among the local and small brewers.

The focus for the smaller and local breweries is that elusive target, brewing the best beer.

ART AND SCIENCE

A stereotypical pic of a local brewer shows a hipster guy with a beard, leaning over a sifter of amber ale or a hazy IPA, with sparkling metal tanks looming behind them.

In reality, brewing takes hard work and hours of cleaning. Brewmasters begin in the early morning hours and stay until after dark.

Brewing is a special craft that combines the extremes of creativity and exact science. At one level, brewing is a simple mix of grains, water, yeast, and other ingredients, but the science to make good beer includes biology, chemistry, and engineering.

You don't get a simple scientific answer from the brewing formula, though. The end product is meant to consume, taste, and enjoy. That takes artistry, creativity, and innovation, especially to make a beverage that is of amazing quality yet distinct from others that have come before.

I can relate to the mastery of brewing as a musician—not that I'm a very good one. There are basics you have to learn before you even begin to play the guitar, such as the fundamentals of frets, tuning, and finger placement. The goal is to make music. We learn how to play the guitar because we want to rock like Eddie Van Halen or another hero. But it's a long way to that from a simple G chord. It takes hours and hours of practice and playing other people's songs.

Once those fundamentals are mastered, then the art comes. We can write our own songs and find our own styles.

However, there is a difference between playing in a living room, where my mom says I rock, and playing music professionally.

The same process happens with brewers. Many begin as homebrewers. But making a decent brew for friends who love free beer is different from scaling up on a pro brew system for the masses who will pay for the beverage. It takes hours of practice and learning from others in a community before becoming an artist who inspires others with a glass of beer.

It takes science and engineering, creativity, resiliency, and mopping.

Why would someone invest all that time—months or years—and energy into making beer?

Because they love it. Like the songwriter who sees the tear in the eye of a listener, the brewer seeks that connection with people who can appreciate the effort, the creativity, and the combination of flavors in a great brew.

Know What to Ignore and What Is Important

Walt Wooden of StillFire is one of those rare people who can work in both worlds of science and artistry. Before brewing full time, his day job was building websites for clients, but he also had experience in graphic design. The hobby of homebrewing appealed to him. He agrees that it takes a special type of person to brew well.

His partner, Phil Ferril, says that to be a good brewer, you have to know what to ignore and what's important. There's always something important going on in the process of brewing. Other things don't matter. He could brew a beer, pitch in some yeast, and sit there measuring and worrying. But at that point, the "cement is in the mold." There's not much he can do. Yeast has made beer for thousands of years. Let it do what it does best.

There are times when certain ingredients don't cooperate, but much of the art is having a gut feeling and making calculated decisions along the way. Every decision has consequences. If you adjust one part of the recipe, there will be a consequence.

When Phil was flying planes as a gunnery in the air force, he operated in combat-style missions. He made his best calculations, but if something landed off to the right or left, short or long, he made the adjustments based on the result, even if he believed he did everything right to begin with.

Pouring the Dropout IPA at StillFire.
Courtesy Karl Lamb.

Brewing is similar. There are so many variables to worry about that it would take forever to get them perfect. At some point, you have to take a shot and adjust to get better.

Walt and Phil come from a homebrewing background, and it was a strange transition. Walt went to college as a chemical engineer and changed his major to art. His brain is half science and half art, which has been a problem for him for most of his life. Sometimes he plays too much and forgets the science, or he geeks out on the science and forgets the art and end goal.

There are four major canons of beer—water, yeast, hops, and grains. Anyone can stir them together and make beer even without knowing what he or she is doing. But when you know what you're doing, something magical happens.

Walt's brother gave him some good advice. He said that when Walt didn't know the answer to a question, he should say he doesn't know and commit to doing the research. When you know how to do the research, you can go further.

The brewers at StillFire did a ton of research and found the right equipment—all the stainless steel and control panels—at the right time. Someone came in and taught them how everything worked. Walt felt like he got a master's degree in those two days to learn everything he needed to know. It was better than four years of college.

Phil has more experience in making beer but admits he doesn't know it all. He learns what he needs when he needs it. Every step in the brewhouse is calculated.

It may be aiming low, but the number-one rule of the operation is that no one gets hurt. So many things happen every day—working with nasty chemicals, pressurized gas, and extreme heat—that the danger is real. Walt admits that he once undid a clamp, and it fired off like a cannon.

The second rule is to be gentle with the equipment. Less stress on hoses and panels means they will break less often.

Phil loves the creativity of brewing and the challenge of being asked if he can make a particular beer. The answer is almost universally yes, but some styles take longer to produce. He might have to do some research or find the right ingredients. He has developed his palate enough that when he tastes a beer, he can tell how to re-create it. It might not always be exact, but it'll be close.

A lot of things are innovative in small ways. Often, styles or beers that people wanted to be trends never took off, such as garlic in IPAs. The customer base didn't like it.

A Brewing Team

A brewery doesn't always need a brewer who is good in both disciplines, the art and the science. It is often good to have a team of people with different backgrounds who bounce ideas off each other and work together.

Slow Pour has a team of four brewers with diverse strengths. Matt Lamattina's culinary background adds ideas about how flavors work together and what should be paired with what. The others on the team include a person with a scientific mind and a young brewer learning the ropes. That is the approach for John Reynolds and Slow Pour to constantly challenge themselves and get a little better each day.

Enjoying brews together in the taproom at Slow Pour.
Courtesy Slow Pour Brewing.

The brewery is uniquely positioned outside the perimeter of Atlanta to make what they want apart from the popular styles. Within Atlanta, the trendy styles, such as the hazy IPAs, sours, and stouts, dominate the breweries. Slow Pour does pay attention and participates in the trends, but they simply get a little more leniency with them.

They are a healthy mix of core styles and innovation. Their core brands are the Cotillion blonde ale and two IPAs, Southernality and Nostalgia. Like many breweries, they rotate seasonals through the product line. Annie Are You Okay is their seasonal barrel-aged stout. With its high alcohol content, if you have a few of those, they'll ask if you're okay. The Honorable is the Dunkel beer.

John and Slow Pour won the Georgia beer prize at the Suwanee Beer Fest soon after they opened. With the new brewers on the team and the constant motivation to get better, they've only excelled since then.

Slow Pour hasn't done any collaborations, and, as an owner, John is more focused on partnerships and integrating the front and back of the brewery in a cohesive experience for the community.

Always Something New to Learn

Matt Glidden grew up on a farm and learned the value of hard work. He didn't apply that value to school as much, however, and it wasn't until opening Ass Clown that he realized the amount of science involved in the process. He should have been sitting in the front row in chemistry class back in school, paying attention, instead of in the back row, he says.

Brewing isn't a job that a person can perfect. Some jobs you can figure out and know like the back of your hand. They become easy, with not much more to learn. In craft beer, there's always something more to learn. That constant need for education actually drew Matt to the industry. He goes to classes on yeast, barrel aging, and souring and is always reading articles. Even when Matt thinks he knows a lot, one beer can change that in a second.

Consumers have become more educated, as well. Years ago, a brewer could get away with an average beer or a style that was not executed well. The craft crowd also tires of drinking the same beers. They want to experience new things.

At his brewery, Matt has four walls with bottles of beer from what he calls "the beer gods"—breweries that make perfect beer. He has collected them as a tribute and displays them for inspiration.

Consistency Requires the Science

The brewer at Port City is very creative after twenty years of experience. Developing new recipes and ways to brew them involve the skills

Snifters waiting for the beer at Ass Clown.
Courtesy LunahZon Photography.

of creativity and artistry. But when the goal is consistency, the science is necessary to repeat the quality and taste time after time.

Port City invested in a quality control lab for the equipment, such as tanks and computer technology. Since Port City also endeavors to distribute, they work on ways to make the beers more consistent and shelf stable so that they will always taste the same, both today and six months from now.

Complexity of Brewing

Dino Radosta brewed the first batch of beer at White Street, but it was terrible. He felt he needed to learn the basics and have those conversations to understand what goes into the process.

He likens a brewer to an artist, a writer, or a chef who understands how different ingredients work. Talent alone doesn't make a good

Mixing and prepping at Port City.
Courtesy Port City Brewing.

brewer though. It takes practice to develop the necessary skills to make great beer.

Making beer isn't hard. The Egyptians did it by accident. Even making decent beer isn't that hard, and with a little effort and practice, a person can make a good product.

But making the same exact good beer every single time is exceedingly difficult. Dino considers people who can do that brewmasters.

Craft people can mock the big conglomerates, but Dino has never tasted a beer from one of the big brewers that didn't taste exactly the same as every other one. They taste identical, and that's hard to do.

Like anything in life, if people work hard, they get better. The struggle for some is when the novelty wears off and they realize it's hard work. They'll have to learn about mundane things like hop contracts. Does that brewer have the work ethic to push through? Once brewers get past "your stuff's not that bad," they need resiliency and diligence.

Prepping the tanks at White Street.
Courtesy White Street Brewing.

White Street also employs a team approach. They have not just a brewer but also a chemist who knows what ingredients do and an engineer who can fix equipment when it breaks and understands pressure and gases. The complexity of brewing is mind-boggling. One of the primary ingredients is a living organism, yeast, so the brewer has to know biology and understand how to make that living organism behave.

Now the brewer also works in an environment that's government regulated, with a product that easily spoils. That's a complex process.

Passion for the Creativity

Shaun Yasaki's passion comes from the creative side of brewing, although he also has a tech mind and enjoys managing the facility, pumps, boilers, and other mechanical aspects. The brewing is a great creative outlet.

Feeling that there's sometimes too much innovation in craft brewing (five random ingredients shoved in a stout, for example), at Noble Beast, he gravitates to the traditional styles and making them well, creating a beverage people like to drink. As an example, he wanted to make a Bohemian pilsner, so he went out of the way to get full-malted barley, which he had to import from Moravia. The hops were brought in from Eastern Europe. He designed the brewhouse himself, and it uses an older method of mashing. To Shaun, re-creating that pilsner as closely as possible was as challenging—if not more so—as making some off-the-wall beer.

A brewmaster is like a head chef. There's almost a celebrity element to it, like those legendary chefs who create dishes. Shaun has brewer friends who are very creative but not as skilled at the technical side. Others are the opposite—they are technical and can tell you about hump curves, but sometimes their beers come across as boring or one-dimensional. Somewhere in the middle is a happy medium for brewing.

Creativity takes other forms too, such as in naming the beers. Sometimes a brewer gets an inspiration for a beer name and loves it. Other times, finding a name is a pain. Shaun has a list on his phone of over two hundred beer names. When he hears something that he thinks would be a great beer name, he adds it to the list, and he can go back to it when he needs a new moniker.

There isn't much creativity involved in making traditional German style beers, which Shaun especially loves. They are very technical and process driven; the recipe is what it is. What proves his chops is how he can execute all the elements of the process well, going above and beyond. Learning about water chemistry also plays a big role.

In the end, it is satisfying when a beer is well executed and tastes amazing.

In the Zone

There are moments, as a musician, when the music carries me along, and I'm not thinking about what I'm playing, but every note and transition was perfect. Sports figures talk about those games where they can't miss a shot and aren't planning the next move but they're always in the perfect place and make the right play.

They call it being "in the zone."

It happens with brewers too.

Brewers who are more scholarly say they wish they were more artistic. The artists wish they knew more about the science. It depends on where they are in their brewing careers, but they all begin with the fundamentals of how things operate. The more that the basics become second nature for them, the more art is involved. The more comfortable brewers are with elements such as hops, yeast, and grains, the more able they are to start creating the tastes they want.

They get into the zone.

Consistency doesn't come into play for brewers when the brewery is small and doing one-offs. In some markets, not having the same beer each time is an advantage. Some consumers don't want to drink the same beer twice. The brewery needs to know its market and model, especially in an industry with a drop-off of brand loyalty and people who are looking for great beer and new experiences.

Brewing as a Canvas

Neil Fisher of WeldWerks never considered himself much of a creative person until he started brewing.

Brewing was a canvas he had never thought of before, using ingredients and recipes as paints to design something new and unique.

However, beer is also a manufactured product in a manufacturing industry. A homebrewer doesn't have to worry about shelf stability or consistency or efficiency. The homebrewer doesn't worry about the market. When one graduates to being a pro brewer, the brewery must consider what it sells.

In the brewhouse at WeldWerks.
Courtesy WeldWerks Brewing.

Brewers have to be careful with the manufacturing aspect. When it becomes about efficiency and profit, those concerns can suck the soul out of a product. But if a brewery goes to the other extreme of creativity and artistry without considering other details, the business fails and closes. There has to be balance.

In WeldWerks' first year, Neil admits to their lack of knowledge. They first took time to dial in the quality. After they cleared that important hurdle, then they learned what to make.

Innate Ability

Chuck Comeau of Liquid Bread says that sometimes we meet people with an innate ability to understand and translate something. He believes that his brewer, Brendan Arnold, has that ability. He just understands beer.

Back with the tanks at Liquid Bread.
Courtesy Liquid Bread Brewing.

Beer involves disciplines like microbiology and chemistry. Brewers must love those aspects, or it doesn't work. Brewmasters are part mad scientists to make great beer. When people do it as a job or because they think it's cool, it doesn't work. The brewer has to have the right sensibilities to begin with.

Talent alone doesn't cut it either. Brendan has a love and passion for brewing, which is always important. Brewmasters believe that if you're going to do something, then you must commit to excellence. Brendan takes classes and courses and has nearly completed an advanced brewing theory certificate.

Time is the test to see how much brewmasters love what they're doing. Does time pass quickly when they brew day in and day out? That's the test.

Some brewers are like doctors who knows the facts but don't have the right personality or bedside manner. People can talk to those brewers and tell that they don't have the passion.

Brendan considers himself one of the few guys left who likes real beer. With some of the new styles, is it beer anymore? He focuses on a high-quality beer, looking at the underlying science and trying to make the cleanest beer he can.

The industry talks about West Coast or East Coast styles. Being in Kansas, Liquid Bread is trying to lead the pack in the Midwest style. They still filter their beers, while others threw out filters years ago. For Brendan, the difficulty is in producing light, high-quality styles that he can't cover up with dry hopping six pounds per barrel or adding pounds of blueberries, lactose, or vanilla beans. Those might be great beverages, but they aren't as challenging.

Chuck remembers how a fashion designer was known for making beautiful fashion for women, and he was asked about his competitors and how others pushed the envelope. The designer remarked that while he appreciated his competitors and how forward thinking they were, he knew many women with a lot of money who just wanted a pretty dress.

It's the same with beer. Some brewers push the envelope and are way out there, but a lot of people just want a great beer. You don't have to be bizarre to be great. Often, it simply comes down to doing something well.

Checking the tanks at Revolution Brewing.
Courtesy Revolution Brewing.

When musicians play songs, they can add dozens of instruments and all the latest technology to master the product, but you know how you can tell it's a good song? If you can play it on a single instrument, like a guitar or piano, with a vocalist, and it still moves the listener, no matter what style it is.

Making a simple but amazing beer is a masterful challenge.

The Essence of Craft

Josh Deth's father was a scientist, so Josh loves the science aspect of brewing. But he's more of a musician, and the artist part of the process appeals to him as well.

When he was opening Revolution, he dreamed about what he wanted it to be. He could make any kind of beer he wanted, with a diverse array of styles to pick from. Old historical styles are being resurrected, and people are using wacky yeast to get different results. Dry hop or hazy IPAs rip off old European beers.

People in the industry debate about what is and what isn't craft beer. The whole idea of making a small batch and thinking through how it's made is craft at its essence. The brewer infuses care into the product on a small scale, and people can point to the one who made it and the recipe.

At Revolution, the brewer writes his recipes and craft in a spiral notebook with a mechanical pencil, and he still has papers from his days in brewing school. He doesn't use computers as much, preferring to work it out by hand. In many ways, Revolution is high tech, but sometimes the artists like to go old school.

Revolution works with both the small batches at their brewpub and larger amounts at the production facility.

The Brewers' Heaven

The brewers come in at 5:00 a.m., and they brew alone, pouring hops into a tank, feeling the heat. The smell of grain fills their nostrils, and they hear the hum of the pumps and glycol. That is the moment when the brewers know they are using the brewhouse to produce art. It's the brewers' heaven.

Customers arrive and give their gratitude to Brandon Wright for making the beer and giving them a warm feeling in a happy place.

Werk Force is a small brewery with a great deal of creative freedom. Brandon doesn't have to answer to investors to make a particular beer because the numbers look good or to a distributer to make the same beer over and over. He constantly gets to do new and exciting things. A few of his beers are so popular that he can't keep them in stock. When customers ask why a beer isn't available, he answers that he wanted to try something new. They reprint the tap list every day for the twenty-four taps in the brewery.

Brandon still does a majority of the brewing, production, and packaging. He has three workers who operate the barreling and help with the packaging. It's an awesome staff. The homebrew shop is still open but is two spaces down, unconnected, and has a two-barrel system

Brewers' Heaven.
Courtesy Amanda Wright.

that allows him to make sour and wild beer. The clean beer is made at the main brewery.

Many professional brewers started in homebrewing, and Brandon comments on how homebrewing and homeschooling are similar in culture. Homebrewers read books at home, teach themselves brewing, join clubs, and share experiences with others like them. He took that model and learned by reading books and hanging out at breweries, making friends in the industry. Like a sponge, he soaked everything up.

When you're passionate about a subject, he says, there's no better teacher than yourself. If people want to learn, they will find a way.

Yes, it was difficult to learn engineering, biology, and physics, as well as how to solder pipes together or replace electrical connections. When a control panel goes down, he has to call tech support in California, and they talk him through it. A capacitor blew up in the panel once, and blue smoke billowed out; he had to figure out how to get help.

But with passion and love, those struggles were worth it.

Develop the Palate

When Scott Wood opened Courtyard, he wanted to make IPAs. It's not revolutionary now, but no one in New Orleans was making the classic West Coast styles such as hazy IPAs or heavy dry-hopped IPAs with pale malt. Early on, that's what put Courtyard on the map.

Scott went front to back on classic styles as a homebrewer, wanting to make contemporary iterations of styles but needing to know how to make the classics first. The philosophy was that if he could make the classics well, he'd prove his chops and could graduate to the more creative aspects. Others may not agree with or take that approach, but he felt it was important.

They still make classics at Courtyard, but now they brew interesting concoctions such as the Oyster Stout with fresh oysters from the Gulf. They grill half to eat and use the other half for the beer. It's a New Year's Day tradition to have a sack or two of oysters at the brewery with the Oyster Stout. Scott also makes a beer with raspberry honey.

Scott's palate has gone through major transitions since he opened. He takes his son with him to the grocery store to smell fruit, and buys things to see what they taste like—and not just food. Scott's always smelling trees and leaves and dirt, wanting to include those smells and tastes in his library.

When he's describing beers or smelling hops or malt, he has a library of aromatic compounds he can bring. "That's lilac," for example. That library is important for coming up with new ideas and appreciating another brewer's beer.

Of course, that level of detail can go too far and ruin the ability to simply enjoy the beer if he's constantly critiquing it—especially his own beer. He had to back off so that he could drink the beer he brews.

The Magical Spark

"Brewmaster" means different things to different people. Homebrewers come into the industry and call themselves brewmasters. People working at brew schools say you're not a brewmaster unless you have

The massive tanks at La Cumbre.
Courtesy Cory Campbell.

a master's degree in the discipline. The public perception is that the brewmaster spends time walking around tanks and tasting beer and is flamboyant and artsy.

Jeff Erway at La Cumbre defines a brewmaster as the person in any facility who deals with the business and details of ingredients. "Gentleman brewer" is another term, but it's not his favorite.

He was a good cook for most of his life, passionate about the food but not the science. It took getting into craft brewing to become interested in the science aspects.

As a musician himself, he combined the creativity of jazz and cooking with the mystic alchemy of fermentation and created a magical spark. He also loved the history. Brewers are literally part of a ten-thousand-year-old chain of tradespeople who made beer. In brewing, he's experienced moments of epiphany traveling around trying beers that were like the first time he heard Pink Floyd's *Dark Side of the Moon*. These beers weren't just good. They were mind-bendingly good. It was earth-shattering to him, and he wanted to know how to make them.

That passion and experience keeps Jeff going today—the passion to create something that isn't just a beverage to consume but a beer to ponder, a brew so compelling that others would stop to try to dissect it.

In order to get that experience, however, a brewery needs to know how to run a business and make the numbers work. They must keep the lights on.

THE BIZ

Business can kill passion.

Deep desires fuel the dream to open a local brewery—the desire to make great beer, see community happen, be an artist and an innovator, express your beliefs, connect with the rich history of the past, tell stories, and be a part of an amazing movement. All this is wrapped up in the perfect job where you can make money doing what you love.

That's where things get interesting—the making-money part.

The craft industry might be unique in its redefinition of success, in that there is room for everyone, and the goal isn't to crush the competition but to live and let live and even generously collaborate in business. However, a brewery still needs to make money to stay open, pay the light bills, and keep employees. That necessitates some level of business sense and attention to detail.

Where will you get ingredients? How much are you willing to pay? The margin in craft beer, especially in the taproom, is more advantageous than in other high-quality industries such as slow food, but those margins can be consumed quickly with hop contracts or electric bills or poorly trained employees.

The topic of saturation kept coming up in conversations with brewers and owners. The industry is in an interesting transition. After years of growth, even during the worst economic downturn since the Great Depression, expansion has slowed. Breweries that were once legendary are closing, and the recent COVID-19 pandemic is forcing local breweries to be creative in the midst of great uncertainty.

Is saturation to blame for the slowdown? Are there too many breweries, or is the industry simply making an adjustment that is common to all industries? The people in the trenches have their perspectives.

Big companies, looking to make money on this "new craft beer thing," came along with the growth. Conglomerates got rid of the competition by buying smaller companies and making them part of the empire or closing them down. As you can imagine, that caused resentment and skepticism in a culture that was built on extreme collaboration.

It isn't only the big companies either. Local businesses with cash to invest dream of distribution and cans or bottles of their brands on the shelves of grocery and liquor stores. Does that betray the foundation of being local and craft?

In this context, local brewers work for hours to create amazing beers that reflect their individual styles, connect with and give back to the community, and keep their heads from dropping below the water.

In the end, the business is about the beer. Even if you have great marketing and business acumen, bad beer won't cut it. Even average beer won't cut it anymore.

It's still about great beer.

Keep the Regionals Alive

In 2018, national brewers were flat in relation to growth. The heritage breweries, such as Sierra Nevada, Sam Adams, or New Belgium, declined in sales. Only two of the top ten grew.

There are reasons for that, not the least of which is what the big conglomerates have done to the market. The conglomerates haven't affected the local craft breweries that are making a living in their taprooms. However, the regional and distributing breweries have been affected by the larger domestic beer companies targeting their marketing, competing with them, and simply buying a few of the regional breweries.

Jeff Erway from La Cumbre believes that craft brewing needs those regional brewers. Those larger, regional breweries become incubators for the industry. People work there, learn quality and consistency, and

The complicated work of brewing at La Cumbre.
Courtesy Cory Campbell.

then move on to become head brewers elsewhere or open their own breweries. Those regional breweries are examples of success.

Someone with little or no experience brewing on a commercial scale will often open a brewery and become an emperor with no clothes, not ready for the immense challenges. Jeff credits his ability to creating great beer on his own to the six months he took learning under an amazing, more experienced brewer.

It would be a shame if the regional breweries are lost. They might not create the type of community that people desire in the local cities or towns, but they employ the most people and invest in new technology. They help universities create brewing schools that teach the brewers of tomorrow.

The craft market is growing tighter, and companies such as Anheuser Busch grow where there isn't a strong craft presence, especially in the South. But there are other reasons for the slower growth.

People between the ages of twenty-one and twenty-five drink half as much beer as those of the previous generation did at the same age. They participate in conspicuous consumption at a higher rate, paying for products they believe give prestige. With social media, the young want an Instagrammable experience. For breweries now, success is increasingly determined by their social media savvy and branding.

Beer, in general, has been on the decline for the last twenty-five years. Craft beer bucked that trend for a while, but now an adjustment is happening. Young people are drinking more seltzers, wine, and liquor. Those sectors are growing.

It is also important to recognize the increase of marijuana use. More states are legalizing the drug, and it is losing its negative association. It's another option for more young people.

The craft market is going through a phase of correction, which means that the industry will have to be wise and batten down the hatches. Through all the good years, some brewers possibly got a little overzealous and expanded too quickly, thinking the rate of growth would continue. It hasn't. There will be more corrections in the next five years. Jeff hopes the industry doesn't lose the breweries that built the industry.

Those regional breweries sell 80 percent of the craft beer sold in grocery stores, and the money in the industry is dependent on that distribution. La Cumbre had a great 2011–2012, and when they started distributing, the market was very receptive to introducing a world-class IPA. Customers were waiting for a local brewery to create a high-quality IPA with a lot of flavor. La Cumbre instantly developed high demand in Albuquerque and Santa Fe. With 114 accounts in 2014, they couldn't make enough beer.

That growth lasted into 2016. La Cumbre's distribution entered Colorado, and a few customers no longer considered them "local." But the breweries that took advantage of that period of growth got a leg up at the right time to have a foothold in the market.

Buying local has been highly important for a long time, and products have even become hyperlocal. La Cumbre distributes to Arizona and Colorado, but Jeff understands when people want a great local option. His brewery benefits from that too. Why wouldn't they want beer on tap? It tastes amazing and fresh that way.

There is stiff competition for the regionals as well, but it's not a blood-bath. Regional breweries need representation by great salespeople.

Some buck trends. Others find irrational exuberance (hype) around a new brand.

Small breweries need a good product, money to open, and a team of people to run it successfully. If your goal is to have a nice taproom and make a good living for you and your family, there's plenty of room in the market for that. But growing a large brand will be tough.

Jeff counts himself lucky that he has a CFO who says "no." In the middle of all that growth, some breweries contracted hops based on those numbers over the next five or six years and are now in a multimillion-dollar hole with hop brokers and can't do anything with all those hops since the industry slowed down. Others took out loans for huge production facilities, such as $10 to $15 million for a brewhouse capable of making 100,000 barrels a year, but now they're only making 50,000. The demand isn't there for the beer anymore, but they have huge loan payments they need to make before they pay for any other expenses.

With those problems, some breweries have gone under. That is unfortunate, but it's part of the natural progression of the industry.

Jeff opened with $400,000 and had $80 left in his bank account. La Cumbre opened because it had to. The paint wasn't even dry on the walls. Fortunately, Jeff had a reputation for good beer. That was all he had. If that beer had been bad, he would have failed.

They could have gone out of business several times in the first six months, but he had a business partner who schooled the brewery on finances. La Cumbre made it. Many breweries need more than that today to make it, although it depends on their locations. A brewery in Georgia would be different than Denver, for instance.

Jeff remembers a brewery that opened three years ago. The men were older, in their early sixties, and well financed. Those men believed that if they had enough money, a good brewer, and some business experience, they would make it. They didn't think the brand was important. It looked like 1990s' clip art, and the brewery was nonexistent on social media.

They thought all their friends would come in. Their friends were also sixty and drank half what they did when they were forty. Forty-year-olds drink half what they did at twenty-one. This brewery was marketing to people who drink less and less often and prefer to stay at home.

A brewery's target audience is twenty-one- to twenty-five-year-olds because they always replenish themselves. Jeff felt terrible for that brewery. They lost a ton of money and failed.

Stay the Course

It will be like what happened in the wine industry, Chuck Comeau of Liquid Bread says. Small vineyards produced beautiful wines, and then people found it enjoyable to start their own vineyards, buy grapes, and add their own signatures. After the trend came and went, a handful of people survived who still made great wine.

The same will happen with craft beer. People get into the industry for a myriad of reasons, but the ones who survive will be those who consistently make great beer, regardless of trends. That's why they got into the business in the first place.

With so many breweries out there, the market will adjust, and some will close. Any market that has more product than demand goes through the same correction. What's the solution? Stay the course. Do what you know and what you really enjoy. Push the envelope and create beer that people love and that leads to great experiences.

Continuing on has taken more creativity during the COVID-19 pandemic, however, necessitating new avenues to communicate with customers, create community, and give back to those in need.

Growth can be a trap. When a brewery is small, like Liquid Bread is, the focus can be on a hands-on approach for the highest quality possible. Once the beer is put in a bottle or a can, the beer starts to go downhill.

It takes six months to get it on the shelf, so by the time it gets to market, it's not what the brewer intended. How do you keep a fresh, high-quality product on the market? Brendan Arnold doesn't believe you can. Keeping it on draft and in as close proximity as possible is the key. The only time Liquid Bread has been out there with distribution was a collaboration with another beer.

A great brew at Liquid Bread.
Courtesy Liquid Bread Brewing.

A board of directors governs Liquid Bread, and, fortunately, it is in favor of keeping things small and of the highest quality. Sometimes the brewery can't produce quickly enough, and other times it can.

Making the best possible beer is important to staying in the market. If a brewery can stay the course with quality, the market will eventually come back. How does a brewery get real feedback by going big? Doing what they think is right will usually be the most productive.

Not Always Sexy or Fun

Neil Fisher of WeldWerks cautions that if you just like to make beer, stay a homebrewer. So much more goes into opening a brewery—way more than just making beer.

The business isn't always sexy or fun. Neil hasn't brewed in over a year. Since he has so many talented people working for him, he handles the day-to-day operations. That can be disheartening for brewers who love brewing and making great beers. Opening a brewery might not be the best answer for them.

Validation came for Neil after winning the homebrewing medals. Those accolades convinced him and Colin Jones to open the brewery, but they really had no idea what they were doing. If they had, maybe they wouldn't have done it. They weren't ready for the workload.

The first step to success, however, is to make a product that stands on its own. As stated earlier, Neil and Colin took the first year to dial in quality and the second to learn what they wanted to make. WeldWerks later contracted with another brewery to start the canning line. It was a great relationship, but it limited them. Cutting costs led to lower quality. Canning got them away from what made them unique—quality and innovation.

In 2018, they started to make short-run, experimental beers in addition to the existing lines, getting them back to focusing on quality and innovation.

Matt Glidden from Ass Clown agrees with the focus on quality and innovation. If people aren't making good quality beer, they won't survive. He's not worried about the competition if another brewery opens down the street. Ass Clown has set the bar really high with the quality

Canning at WeldWerks.
Courtesy WeldWerks Brewing.

of their beers. The new brewery might brew a great beer, and if they do, they deserve to build a customer base.

There's no reason consumers should tolerate bad beer. There are too many great options out there.

In It for the Right Reasons

Brandon Wright and Werk Force put all their money back into the business and moved into a bigger space. But the finances can sometimes surprise you.

Hard work in the brewhouse at Werk Force.
Courtesy Amanda Wright.

One year, after some growth, the accountant praised the brewery for a great year. Werk Force was profitable. Brandon took a paycheck. But because of the growth, he now owed $40,000 in federal and state taxes.

Shocked, Brandon explained that he didn't have that much money. He had put all the profit back into the business. He learned that the cost of goods isn't an expense—technically, it's income. He scrambled for the $40,000 and survived.

Brandon's story is full of zoning and real estate issues, managing finances and employees, financing, and tax liabilities. Those have helped shape the future as much as the passion for making great beer has—if not more.

The increased saturation of the market means that a brewery can't be the next Budweiser. but that isn't the goal anyway. Breweries have to be satisfied with being local and community driven. If you're in it for the money, you won't last long.

If you want to have a forty-hour work week and have weekends free, don't get into brewing. Brandon is ecstatic when he has an eighty-hour work week. He feels like he's on vacation at that point.

He was having lunch one day with the other brewers in the taproom, and they talked about forums and Facebook groups that exist solely for brewers to complain about their jobs. Some of them are funny. Others complain about getting in at 5:30 a.m. to clean a tank. The brewers agreed that those people shouldn't be in the business. When Brandon comes in at 5:00 a.m., cleans a tank, and gets ready for a brew, he loves what he's doing.

You're in it for the wrong reasons if you want the label of being a brewer, Brandon says. Brewers are involved in hard custodial work most of the time, scrubbing stainless steel twenty-four hours a day. That's the job. Beers reflect all that work and passion. If you're not willing to put in the work, it's going to show in the product.

Learning Curve

In many ways, a brewery is like any business, with costs, price points, and good customer service so people will want to come back. Josh Deth at Revolution believes it is important to treat the employees well, to ensure that they want to work for him. Marketing is also a growing necessity to stand out in the industry.

Dealing with distribution, quality, and consistency is paramount. Problems with quality are natural, especially when brewing different styles of beer, so Revolution invests a great deal of money and time in quality and consistency.

Matt Glidden's background is in mortgages, and some of the principles of that business carry over. However, breweries are a different ball game, and it was difficult to adapt. He has kept Ass Clown small, not wanting to jump in over his head with contracts or extreme expansion.

The effect of saturation has been a movement to push more local. Matt doesn't pasteurize or filter beer, believing that unfiltered product the real state of beer, as it is in the UK. If it's not treated right, he jokes, the beer might come back to life. Filtering strips flavor and body

Kegs from Revolution ready to go out.
Courtesy Revolution Brewing.

out of the beer, including some elements that are good for you, such as vitamin B12.

While Matt has tried not to overextend himself, he isn't scared to take risks with beers. He learns from every beer he makes, whether it doesn't sell or gets great Untappd reviews. Each beer teaches him things that work or don't. He remembers a wasabi oyster beer they had to dump, but failure is part of learning.

However, the beer industry is less forgiving now than it was years ago. Consumers are better educated about great beer and don't tolerate mistakes. Matt has to run a tight ship, and if there's any doubt about

At Ass Clown, business is relationships.
Courtesy LunahZon Photography.

a beer, they have to fix it before it goes out to the public. That's an advantage of being small—the mistakes don't create the same damage they might with a larger brewery.

Demand in Front of Supply

When the owner and the brewer are two different people, their relationship is central to success. Owners who don't listen to their brewers have issues staying profitable and keeping up with demand. They must listen to the people making the products and understand that quality takes precedence to accessibility, marketing, and the rest.

The model is that demand should always be in front of supply. Thomas Mercado at Rock Bottom in Nashville runs out of beer every now and then. He doesn't want to run out all the time, but he also doesn't want too much supply. The brewery has to strike a balance and be flexible.

That doesn't mean marketing isn't important. Craft beer has a message. A brewery has to have something to say, and if they can't communicate that message, the brewery peters out.

Some of the popular craft brands are shrinking because more breweries are entering the industry, but a higher percentage of breweries are lasting. The breweries that fail are trying to overreach with wide and shallow marketing instead of deep and local. Some lessons are learned the hard way. A recent brewery filed bankruptcy, but Thomas and others saw it coming due to bad decisions about quality control and overextended distribution. It's not the way to make money anymore.

Need a Team

Since getting the business aspect right is a necessity, John Reynolds and Slow Pour have brought in a team. They are keenly aware of what they don't know and try to partner with people who know better than they do. Pride in areas of business is a recipe for disaster, and Slow Pour has built the team over the last few years—an accountant for the books, someone to manage bar schedules, and someone to look at data comparing growth from last year to predict and adjust.

Slow Pour tries to bring in people with better skills than anyone else in the brewery. The brewery is still building that team and putting those pieces in place. Some employees are wearing too many hats, but Slow Pour is moving closer to where they want to be in that regard.

The people they hire must believe in the vision of the brewery, all marching toward the same goal. At the same time, each person should have the freedom to excel in their respective role. John wants to keep as many talented people on the journey and say, "Come play in the sandbox."

No One in Their Right Mind

If someone who is a great homebrewer who makes amazing beer decides to open a brewery, it will be a tough road ahead if they don't understand the business.

Brewing is fun, but the bank and the ingredient companies want their money.

It is the joke at White Street brewhouse. Lying on the floor on broken glass with hands covered in grease trying to take apart the labeler because a gear came off—they say that moment is in the appendix of "So you want to be a brewer?"

No one in their right mind says they are dying to get into hop contracts, package sourcing, and shelf-space placement.

Years ago, your friends or mom saying you make great beer would have been sufficient, but today the market has changed. Do you want to open a two-barrel brewhouse, sell by the pint in a taproom, and make a living? You can do that without much of a business background. Beyond that, a brewer has to understand how to run a business.

Sam Adams commercials give people the impression that brewing is a bunch of bearded guys leaning next to stainless steel tanks, drinking and laughing, but there's a real business going on. It's a good thing those who aren't good at business aren't crowding the space in the retail market.

Dino Radosta believes there's room in the craft industry for the small local brewery that survives and maintains. The trouble comes when breweries expand too quickly without understanding what it takes to be distributers.

Brewing is a lot of hard work. Great brewing takes even more work. The world has changed over the last thirty years, and hard work isn't valued as it once was. The younger generation isn't entering the industry as much as it used to. Many have the perspective that everything gets done sitting behind a computer. A lot can be done with software and social media, no doubt, but jobs exist that support the brew staff, and these are often paths to becoming a brewer. It is increasingly difficult to find those with the right ethic to work their way into the industry.

Inspecting the tanks at White Street.
Courtesy White Street Brewing.

Pop-Up Brewery

Some people can't stop opening breweries just for fun.

Whit Baker helped open Bond Brothers, a separate brewery nearby, and a third virtual brand with a partner. The virtual pop-up brand, Ancillary Fermentation, is an online brewery that offers beer that is more experimental, experiential, and strange.

It's the dumbest thing they could do, businesswise—they only wholesale beer and have a three-hour pop-up for each beer release once a month. They brew one or two batches a month, and it's a fun way to raise money. They've sold beers such as a juicy IPA called Altered Perception and a fake kettle sour called Liquid Night Show. The beers were released at an event in a rented church with a liquid light show and acid rock band.

Ancillary Fermentation also partnered with a local hotel and made two beers based on their signature cocktails, Movement and Footwork, selling the beers through people holding beer cans and performing interpretive dance and slow yoga.

The virtual store isn't a moneymaker; it's just for fun.

Noble Intentions

Scott Wood at Courtyard knows many people who start breweries with noble intentions. Friends tell them, "You should sell this; it tastes great!" However, most of those people with noble intentions don't want to start a business.

The San Diego craft industry was a test market for large multinational breweries testing different packaging and products. Their way of research and development is drastically larger and less personal.

If Courtyard makes fifteen different beers in a two-month span, they get immediate feedback from customers. Was it good? Bad? It isn't on the scale of the other companies, but the feedback loop is quick and allows for flexibility. When a new style comes out, Scott can make it and see if he enjoys it. He doesn't have to wait for market research or a marketing department to sign off on it. That freedom is immeasurable to him. Courtyard reserves money and resources to allow for that creativity.

Brewers need to choose the path they will take—they either chase growth or chase creativity. What they choose determines what people experience at a personal level in their taprooms.

Choosing what to make, what contracts to sign, and where to take the business are all questions that get into something more difficult to define.

The future.

THE FUTURE

The craft beer industry is clearly in transition. What that transition means depends on who you talk to.

Where I live, in Georgia, the laws that made local breweries more viable changed only recently. The culture, stuck in domestic beer domination and old Prohibition religious thinking, has begun to recognize the value of a local brewpub. Saturation won't be an issue for a few years yet.

While the overall growth of craft beer has slowed or flatlined in the last couple years, new breweries are still opening in places such as Colorado, where there's a small brewery in every small town. Colorado's perspective of what it takes for a new brewery to enter the industry and sustain itself is different than in Georgia, where small cities are opening their doors to the local brewery. Grocery stores only have so much shelf space for those interested in distribution, so the resulting competition is threatening the collaborative foundation of the craft revolution.

The rise of technology and streaming videos means that new homebrewers don't need a community as much as they did before. They can buy equipment online, watch a clip on YouTube, and make adjustments alone.

The founders of the craft revolution are retiring or passing on, leaving behind a legacy, and often the breweries they founded fail without their personalities behind them. Who will grab the torch? With all these transitions, will craft beer continue to be a people's movement, or will it lose the unique counterculture and character?

In the 1990s, when grunge and other styles began selling millions of albums, I joked, "Is it still alternative music if everyone is listening to it?" Craft beer is facing the same question.

At the same time, these transitions and adjustments may lead the way for more innovation and an industry that is stronger than ever.

Everyone wants to know the future, but predictions are difficult to make. What do the people in the industry think will happen? Where is it all going?

Room for Everyone

Questions abound as the market matures after double-digit growth for so long. Many in the industry have become complacent, which is common after so much success, but that level of growth isn't sustainable forever. The third year of less than 5 percent growth has passed, and breweries have started to tighten their belts. The market is changing more than some thought it would.

The row of barrels at WeldWerks. *Courtesy WeldWerks Brewing.*

Without question, the COVID-19 pandemic has brought more chaos to the process, just like it has for many small businesses in almost every industry, raising even more questions. Creating community is difficult when in a lockdown or under strict social distancing guidelines. More breweries have adopted outside eating areas, added canning and growlers for take-home orders, and initiated other creative solutions to survive.

The craft brew industry is all about staying connected to the local community, and many breweries have been heavily involved in bringing relief and charity to those who have lost jobs or need food. One brewer I'm connected with (near me in Duluth, Georgia) began cooking soup and giving it away to the hungry when our nation partially locked down in March and April.

Neil Fisher of WeldWerks believes that for breweries to thrive, not just survive, they need to be nimble. Whether they are big or small, the advantage is in staying agile and continuing to make products the consumer is excited about.

Hard seltzer, for example, seems like it has come out of nowhere. How will that fit in? To never make it seems shortsighted. Seltzer isn't Neil's passion, but he never thought he'd be making hazy IPAs either, and definitely not as much as they were in 2019. Seltzer is going to have a big effect on breweries, and hazy IPAs will continue to grow.

The hardest balance to find is a way to stay relevant in the market while also being true to who you are as a brewer without compromise. Every brewer will have a different answer to that question.

Neil hates the cancel culture on the internet, especially the judgment among others in the craft beer space. Many once hated the hazy IPAs and became critics. Neil sees the same attitude towards the seltzers. The loudest critics are often the ones who are most heard.

If a product doesn't work for you, that's fine, but there has to be room for everyone. Neil can't believe that the people who considered themselves innovators ten years ago are now so critical. Craft beer is built on the premise that there is a place for everything.

The Bubble Is Beginning to Burst

There are signs that the craft beer bubble is beginning to burst. There are more auctions online for brewing equipment. Other brewers are selling out to bigger companies. Consolidation also happens.

Dino Radosta of White Street Brewing believes there will be a stage where the industry can't feed any more people. Local breweries cannibalize their own sales. Why would a bar next door want to carry a brewpub's beer and send customers their way? With mobile canning, any brewery can package its product, and grocery stores are jumping on the "local craft beer" bandwagon. Grocery stores only have so much shelf space, however. The market is definitely tightening up.

Looking ahead, Dino sees two different waves occurring. First, some breweries will go out of business. Second, others will scoop up the cheap equipment, believing that they can do better.

The market will settle at a point where a few will remain who take it seriously and do it right—trying to be good businesses in their communities while making quality products.

Need a Plan

Phil Ferril of StillFire brewed with a friend, a former homebrewer who is now working commercially, and the friend commented that while there has been consolidation, it hasn't affected the bottom end of people coming into the industry as local small breweries.

It is an interesting time, but it's not a good time to turn a hobby into a business without a plan. Twenty-five years ago, if you made beer and it didn't chew up the concrete when you poured it on the ground, you could do okay in the craft industry. There was little to no competition.

Phil and his partner, Walt Wooden, went to a liquor store to do market research and noticed a huge selection of amazing products. Brewers today must be fresher and more accessible in more ways, and with options only growing, differentiating yourself will be more important than ever.

Great brews at StillFire.
Courtesy Karl Lamb.

As a result of the growth and availability of craft beer, homebrewing is wavering. Many used to get into the hobby to make beer they couldn't get elsewhere. Now there is so much great beer available. Do they want to go through the trouble of making beer when they can get it so easily? Is the time and hard work worth it?

Walt wonders if the only possible reason for young people to get into homebrewing is when they can't get alcohol legally but can purchase homebrewing equipment and ingredients. Other than that, the only motivation is the love of the process and experience. The need to make beer you can't get elsewhere is gone for most homebrewers.

At modern homebrewing competitions, the batch size has been reduced to one gallon. Those unable to commit to a whole five-gallon batch usually put the ingredients into an appliance and let the machine make the beer.

Phil also sees a generational shift. People under thirty find a YouTube video, watch for thirty minutes, think they have all the experience they need, and move on to the next subject. The younger generation dabbles instead of fully committing. Not as many of the younger generation are getting into brewing. There's no immediate feedback.

This is a generation who can fight Mike Tyson but doesn't learn to box. They play Guitar Hero without learning to play the guitar and make music. Acquiring those real skills takes time and resiliency, and those things build character, which explains the amazing character of the people in the craft beer industry.

Moving Toward More Community

Amid all the transitions, one of the trends is to move toward a more communal experience, where the beer is the tool that brings the community together celebrates local businesses and personality. Laws prohibiting brewpubs have all but disappeared, and more consumers are searching for local options. That will be an advantage for the neighborhood brewery. It will also be a limitation, since most neighborhoods will only support one or two local breweries.

Whit Baker at Bond Brothers believes that the trend is the third-wave coffee shop model of a unique local business and space where people go for a sense of community and to enjoy quality beverages, but breweries will cover the afternoon and evening instead of the morning.

Matt Glidden with Ass Clown sees the saturation but thinks that breweries on every corner can also be a good thing. Several towns and states thrive with the business and tax dollars a local brewery brings to the area. He looks at Portland, Oregon, or the state of Colorado, where there is a brewery on every block, but they're not hurting or shutting their doors.

Saturation shouldn't be a problem if everyone focuses on themselves and on being unique. Ass Clown brews bold, unique, and odd beers; Northeast IPAs; and sours. Other breweries have their unique styles as well.

More local breweries will mean that the larger breweries, whether craft or conglomerates, will be impacted because the local options will take a larger share of the market, which has already begun happening.

Consumers are looking for more community at Slow Pour.
Courtesy Slow Pour Brewing.

A Brewery in Every Town

John Reynolds from Slow Pour doesn't know if the industry is saturated. In Georgia and in other southern states, it isn't. The importance of having spaces where people can experience the history and character of that town, and food and drink are the primary ways consumers get the local flavor. Until there's a unique local brewery in every town, the industry isn't oversaturated.

John sees the same trend. The industry is less about the styles of beer and more about being hyperlocal and finding the local "watering hole." That makes large craft breweries such as Sweetwater or Creature Comfort less likely to begin and succeed, but the neighborhood breweries will improve their connection and influence in the community.

Good beer is still the price of entry. Great beer gets you in the door. Then you need to decide what you're going to do with it. A consequence of increased options is that standing out becomes more difficult. Having a large distribution network is more of a challenge.

It goes back to changing the idea of success. Larger distribution might have more barriers, but if the goal is to open a place for people to gather and create community while the brewer and owner live comfortably, it's completely possible.

John sees transitions, not saturation.

Shake-Ups

Staying small and local is fine with Brandon Wright and Werk Force. He wants to maintain the ability to be creative and connect with the community.

There are brewers who get into the industry with a passion for great beer versus others who are investor driven and trying to make

Continuing to work hard at Werk Force.
Courtesy Amanda Wright.

money. People saw the craft boom a few years ago and threw money at projects, and some of those failed because the passion wasn't there. Consumers are more educated than ever and can tell when brewers produce something they believe in. That leads to shake-ups in the industry, separating those brewing for the right reasons from those in it just for money.

Brandon explains that breweries will survive with great beer based on passion and creativity. As others have said, ten years ago, consumers might have tolerated average beer, but they won't any longer. Breweries today need to make excellent products and stand behind them, own any mistakes, and rebound. Those will survive.

Era of Adaptation

New beers and styles make this an interesting time. Along with the arrival of seltzers, the industry is also beginning to see more low-calorie craft beers, superfruit beer with antioxidants, and gose beers that are great post-marathon beers with electrolytes and lower ABV.

Generation Z is a bit more health and body conscious. Beer gets a bad rap in that realm, and it has led to changes in the way people brew.

Craft beer is in an era of adaptation. It might be unfortunate for those who are more traditional, but entire breweries are built around "weird beers" with no shelf life, such as the haze craze, lactose, and vanilla. Thomas Mercado at Rock Bottom in Nashville remembers a brewer friend who said that if the younger generation wants to drink candy, then they will brew candy. For those who want traditional styles, there is a dip in excitement for craft beer, but the demand for the strange beers seems like a small percent of the industry.

Due to the interest in low-calorie beers, Thomas thinks the next trend will be craft lagers and pilsners. Locally, he runs an organization for brewers, New Wort Order, a monthly meeting of local brewers in Nashville. The city didn't have a brewing community like California's or Colorado's, so he started the organization there. A different brewery hosts every month. One meeting, an owner from Wisconsin brought out a six-pack of Miller Lite in front of eighteen craft brewers, and everyone started cheering.

More domestic beer drinkers are being converted to craft brewing, but they still want to drink something light and easy. For those not yet converted, lagers are the perfect olive branch. What if they didn't have to drink Bud Light? They could support local businesses and drink a light beer with their neighbors.

In some ways, this would be a repeat of the German lager craze in the late 1800s that made beer that Americans drank. To grow, craft brewing has to give those inroads, such as better-tasting, high-quality light lagers. Again, the craft culture is founded on the idea that there's room for everyone. People question whether Sierra Nevada is too big to be considered craft beer. Even Thomas's staff looks at him askance if he drinks a Kolsch when he wants a beer but has to drive home.

Some in the craft industry must allow space for the adjustments and adaptations for the industry to continue to grow.

CONCLUSION

Craft beer is going through a transition. Some states are experiencing growth with new markets. Others see fighting for space in crowded areas, with breweries on every corner. Social media and a more educated consumer have both changed the game. Years of growth means that it is more difficult for a brewery to open and distribute in a region.

The COVID-19 pandemic is further threatening businesses and altering the landscape. People have adjusted how they get groceries, watch major motion pictures, participate in education, and more. What will changes mean for the craft brew industry?

Different people react differently. A few aren't worried. They believe the market will adjust and correct. Others see the saturation as an issue that is leading to a decline in the collaborative counterculture that appealed to them years ago.

Maybe the solution to these challenges is the same as the heart of the culture that brought craft beer this far. Perhaps these challenges and transitions are opportunities to once again be creative and innovative. Craft beer didn't adopt the mainstream mindset about competition or cheap products for increased profit. It doesn't need to cower in the face of divisive politics, shallow social media, or a pandemic either. As the craft industry faces these challenges, it can emerge on the other side with a clear message, stronger than it's ever been.

A culture continuing to be divided (by politics, racial injustice, and perspectives on lockdown and masks) needs the message of the craft brew industry like never before. Let's sit down and be friends first. Let's begin together, collaborate, be generous.

And with a more educated consumer base, those that thrive will make the best beer they've ever made. That benefits everyone.

The goal will be the same. Come on in, take a break, sit down with your neighbors, experience a pint of excellent beer, and have some great conversation in an environment unique from anywhere else in the world, a place that belongs to you and your community.

Your local brewery.

NOTES

Chapter 2. The Beer Revolution

1. Taryn Smee, "The Ancient Egyptian Obsession with Beer," *Vintage News*, August 27, 2018, https://www.thevintagenews.com/2018/08/27/ancient-egypt-beer/.

2. Karl E. Campbell, "Beer and Breweries," *Encyclopedia of North Carolina*, 2006, https://www.ncpedia.org/beer-and-breweries.

3. Kevin Damask, "The Original Beer Boom: The History of Brewing Runs Deep in Area," *Juneau County Start-Times*, January 10, 2017, https://www.wiscnews.com/juneaucountystartimes/news/local/the-original-beer-boom-history-of-brewing-runs-deep-in/article_d0f63a3f-f344-578c-b414-4445801526fe.html.

4. Maureen Ogle, *Ambitious Brew: The Story of American Beer* (Orlando: Harcourt, 2006), 4, 15.

5. Damask, "Original Beer Boom."

6. Ogle, *Ambitious Brew*, 30, 31.

7. Lisa Grim, "A Brief History of Beer in Chicago," *Serious Eats*, August 9, 2018, https://drinks.seriouseats.com/2012/01/beer-history-chicago-diversey-siebel-meister-brau-miller-lite-goose-island.html.

8. History Channel, "How Prohibition Created the Mafia," video, accessed November 1, 2019.

9. Ogle, *Ambitious Brew*, 203.

10. Ogle, *Ambitious Brew*, 208–209.

11. Ben McFarland, "The Oxford Companion to Beer Definition of California," *Craft Beer and Brewing*, accessed November 1, 2019, https://beerandbrewing.com/dictionary/T6zmDiI95A/.

12. Tom Acitelli, *The Audacity of Hops: The History of America's Craft Beer Revolution* (Chicago: Chicago Review, 2017), 58–61.

13. *Seattle Magazine*, "The History of Beer in Seattle," November 27, 2018, http://www.seattlemag.com/article/history-beer-seattle.

14. Eric Scigliano, "Here's to Washington's 35-Year-Old Craft-Brewing Industry," *Seattle Times*, October 12, 2017, https://www.seattletimes.com /pacific-nw-magazine/cheers-to-beers/.

FEATURED BREWERIES

If you're close to any of these breweries and are looking for a great place to have a beer, please stop in and have one with some great people. They are listed here according to their order of appearance in the book.

Port City Brewing Company in Alexandria, Virginia
https://www.portcitybrewing.com/

Werk Force Brewing Company in Plainfield, Illinois
https://www.werkforcebrewing.com/

The Courtyard Brewery in New Orleans, Louisiana
https://courtyardbrewery.square.site/

White Street Brewing Company in Wake Forest, North Carolina
https://www.whitestreetbrewing.com/

La Cumbre Brewing Company in Albuquerque, New Mexico
https://www.lacumbrebrewing.com/

Slow Pour Brewing Company in Lawrenceville, Georgia
https://slowpourbrewing.com/

Revolution Brewing in Chicago, Illinois
https://revbrew.com/

Ass Clown Brewing Company in Cornelius, North Carolina
https://assclownbrewing.com/brewery/

Liquid Bread Brewing in Hays, Kansas
https://www.lbbrewing.com/

Noble Beast Brewing Company in Cleveland, Ohio
https://www.noblebeastbeer.com/

StillFire Brewing in Suwanee, Georgia
https://stillfirebrewing.com/

Rock Bottom Restaurant and Brewery in Nashville, Tennessee
https://rockbottom.com/locations/nashville/

WeldWerks Brewery in Greely, Colorado
https://weldwerksbrewing.com/

Bond Brothers Beer Company in Cary, North Carolina
https://www.bondbrothersbeer.com/

BIBLIOGRAPHY

Author's Note

I focused on the culture and character of the craft brew industry for a few reasons. First, those aspects appeal to me; I find the craft beer culture unique and fascinating. Second, a book didn't exist that explored the culture and modern issues facing craft beer. Finally, two books have been written that are already excellent resources for those interested to read an in-depth history of beer in America.

Ambitious Brew by Maureen Ogle has been quoted and lauded since she first published the book in 2006. It is still a great resource about the complicated relationship between beer and the US.

Tom Acitelli wrote *The Audacity of Hops*, a book that focused on the background and evolution of the craft beer industry. The latest revised and expanded edition tells great stories and gives an exhaustive and detailed look at craft beer and the people that shaped it.

I highly recommend both books if you'd like to read more.

Acitelli, Tom. *The Audacity of Hops: The History of America's Craft Beer Revolution.* Chicago: Chicago Review, 2017.

Campbell, Karl E. "Beer and Breweries." *Encyclopedia of North Carolina.* 2006. https://www.ncpedia.org/beer-and-breweries.

Damask, Kevin. "The Original Beer Boom: The History of Brewing Runs Deep in Area." *Juneau County Start-Times*, January 10, 2017. https://www.wiscnews.com/juneaucountystartimes/news/local/the-original-beer-boom-history-of-brewing-runs-deep-in/article_d0f63a3f-f344-578c-b414-4445801526fe.html.

Grim, Lisa. "A Brief History of Beer in Chicago." *Serious Eats*. August 9, 2018. https://drinks.seriouseats.com/2012/01/beer-history -chicago-diversey-siebel-meister-brau-miller-lite-goose-island.html.

History Channel. "How Prohibition Created the Mafia." Video. Accessed November 1, 2019.

McFarland, Ben. "The Oxford Companion to Beer Definition of California." *Craft Beer and Brewing*. Accessed November 1, 2019. https:// beerandbrewing.com/dictionary/T6zmDiI95A/.

Ogle, Maureen. *Ambitious Brew: The Story of American Beer*. Orlando: Harcourt, 2006.

Scigliano, Eric. "Here's to Washington's 35-Year-Old Craft-Brewing Industry." *Seattle Times*. October 12, 2017. https://www.seattletimes.com /pacific-nw-magazine/cheers-to-beers/.

Seattle Magazine. "The History of Beer in Seattle." November 27, 2018. http://www.seattlemag.com/article/history-beer-seattle.

Smee, Taryn. "The Ancient Egyptian Obsession with Beer." *The Vintage News*. August 27, 2018. https://www.thevintagenews.com/2018/08/27 /ancient-egypt-beer/.

M. B. Mooney

M. B. Mooney was in the second grade when his teacher, Mrs. Green, tried to keep him out of trouble by saying, "Why don't you write me a story?" He thought that was the best idea ever, and it's kept him out of trouble ever since. Mooney writes fiction and nonfiction and loves a good brew while he works, whether it's specialty coffee or craft beer, which is the basis for the writing podcast, Brew & Ink. He is the author of *Beer Fest USA* (Indiana University Press). He lives with his amazing wife, three creative kids, and a dog in Suwanee, Georgia.

Check him out on his website: www.mbmooney.com

Listen to the podcast: www.brewandink.com

Follow on Instagram as @authormbmooney and Facebook at www.facebook.com/MooneyMB